"Earn. Save. Give. *is filled with the kind of wisdom we have come to expect from Jim Harnish—practical, biblical, insightful, and relevant."*
—**Lovett H. Weems, Jr.,** Distinguished Professor of Church Leadership; Director, Lewis Center for Church Leadership, Wesley Theological Seminary

"If you want to lead persons to become disciples of Jesus around money, you will not find a better resource than this."
—**Vance P. Ross**, Senior Pastor, Gordon Memorial United Methodist Church; Chairman, Convocation for Pastors of Black Churches of the UMC

"I cannot wait to see how God will use Earn. Save. Give. *to help shape and form deeply committed disciples while giving new understanding to the meaning of stewardship."*
—**Donna Claycomb Sokol,** Pastor, Mt. Vernon Place UMC, Washington DC

"Grounded in sacred Scripture; rooted in the Wesleyan tradition; filtered through thoughtful, careful reason; and verified by practiced Christian living—this book is a gift to the church. Thank you, Jim!"
—**Jorge Acevedo,** Lead Pastor, Grace Church, a multi-site United Methodist congregation

"From the heart of a local church pastor comes this practical application of Wesley's theology of money. Offers a contemporary discussion of how Christians think about and use financial resources."
—**Deborah A. McLeod,** Senior Pastor, Mandarin UMC, Jacksonville

"Harnish's approach puts making disciples at the core and raising money as a by-product. From the children's department to the senior citizens, all persons in any church will benefit from participating in this dynamic four-week venture."
—**Clif Christopher,** President, Horizons Stewardship

Earn. Save. Give.
Wesley's Simple Rules for Money

Earn. Save. Give.
978-1-63088-392-8
978-1-63088-393-5 eBook

Earn. Save. Give. - Large Print Edition
978-1-63088-394-2

Earn. Save. Give. - Leader Guide
978-1-63088-395-9
978-1-63088-396-6 eBook

Earn. Save. Give. - DVD
978-1-63088-397-3

Earn. Save. Give. - Program Guide
978-1-63088-398-0 Flash Drive
978-1-63088-399-7 Download

Earn. Save. Give. - Youth Study Book
978-1-63088-400-0
978-1-63088-401-7 eBook

Earn. Save. Give. - Children's Leader Guide
978-1-63088-402-4

Earn. Save. Give. - Devotional Readings for Home
978-1-5018-0507-3
978-1-5018-0509-7 Package of 25
978-1-5018-0508-0 eBook

For more information, visit www.AbingdonPress.com.

Also by James A. Harnish

A Disciple's Heart

A Disciple's Path

Believe in Me

Converge Bible Studies: Women of the Bible

Journey to the Center of the Faith

Living with the Mind of Christ

Passion, Power, and Praise

Radical Renovation

reConnect

Rejoicing in Hope

Simple Rules for Money

Strength for the Broken Places

You Only Have to Die

JAMES A. HARNISH

EARN. SAVE. GIVE.

Wesley's Simple Rules
for Money

Abingdon Press / *Nashville*

Earn. Save. Give.
Wesley's Simple Rules on Money

Copyright © 2015 by Abingdon Press
All rights reserved.

This book is printed on elemental, chlorine-free paper.

ISBN 978-1-63088-392-8

15 16 17 18 19 20 21 22 23 24 — 10 9 8 7 6 5 4 3 2 1

MANUFACTURED IN THE UNITED STATES OF AMERICA

CONTENTS

INTRODUCTION

IF YOU COULD ASK
FOR ANYTHING

If you could ask God for anything in absolute assurance that you would receive it, what would your request be?

A quick glance at the American pop culture scene suggests that money would be at the top of our wish list, followed in quick succession by success, comfort, and fame, all driven by a relentless desire for something we hope will result in "happiness." It seems that the American dream has been commoditized to consist of wealth and possessions, with the operative word being *more*. We work more hours and pour more human energy into an insatiable desire for more money, more success, more comfort, and more of everything that money can buy.

Most of us can identify with Old Testament scholar Walter Brueggemann, who describes our culture as "a society of 24/7 multitasking in order to achieve, accomplish, perform and possess.... [W]e want more, have more, own more, use more, eat and drink more." The result is "an endless pursuit that is always unsatisfied, because we never have gotten or done enough."[1] If Brueggemann's observation is correct, it doesn't paint a healthy or joyful picture of how we live or what we most deeply desire.

But there is more to our story.

Now and then in the congested traffic of our hyperactive lives, there are quiet moments when we are haunted by a hunger for something deeper, stronger, higher, and longer-lasting than accumulating more wealth and possessions. With T. S. Eliot, we find ourselves asking:

Where is the Life we have lost in living?
Where is the wisdom we have lost in knowledge?[2]

Somewhere along the way, often when we least expect it, we surprise ourselves with an honesty that asks for something else altogether; something no amount of money can buy.

That's what happened for Solomon. Following the death of his father, King David, he had a dream in which God said, "Ask whatever you wish, and I'll give it to you" (1 Kings 3:5). In other words, God asked him the very question that began this introduction.

Unlike most of us, Solomon was wise enough to know what he needed most. He prayed, "Please give your servant a *discerning mind* in order to govern your people and to distinguish good from evil, because no one is able to govern this important people of yours without your help" (1 Kings 3:9, italics added). Some translations use the phrase *understanding heart*. The writers of the Old Testament Proverbs called it *wisdom*. They said, "Get wisdom! Get understanding before anything else" (Proverbs 4:7).

Solomon knew that what he needed more than anything was wisdom, the kind of divine discernment that goes beyond accumulating knowledge and enables us to use the knowledge we have gathered. What he needed, and what we need, is an understanding heart that knows what to do with the wealth and possessions we have accumulated. It's the divine insight to know when enough is enough.

The Hebrew storytellers said that God was pleased with Solomon's request and gave him all that he asked for and more, saying:

"Because you have asked for this instead of
requesting long life, wealth, or victory over
your enemies—asking for discernment so as
to acquire good judgment—I will now do just
what you said. Look, I hereby give you a wise
and understanding mind....I now also give you
what you didn't ask for: wealth and fame. There
won't be a king like you as long as you live. And
if you walk in my ways and obey my laws and
commands, just as your father David did, then I
will give you a very long life." (1 Kings 3:11-14)

As the old Gershwin song says, "Who could ask for
anything more?"[3]

MONEY MATTERS

Questions regarding how much money we want,
have, or need are critically important to the way we
live. There is no inherent goodness in poverty or
inherent evil in wealth. Scripture is clear that "the
love of money"—not the money itself—"is the root
of all kinds of evil" (1 Timothy 6:10). My assumption
is that just about everyone reading this book either
could use or would like to have a little more money,
wealth, and possessions. How we earn, save, and give
really matters.

Money matters for our souls.

There is more to our relationship with money than merely balancing our accounts, paying our taxes, and counting our earnings and losses. The temptation to become "rich in things and poor in soul"[4] is always with us.

The Bible is clear that there is a spiritual element in our relationship with our possessions. Jesus personified wealth, saying, "No one can serve two masters....You cannot serve God and wealth" (Matthew 6:24). Paul warned Timothy, "Some have wandered away from the faith and have impaled themselves with a lot of pain because they made money their goal" (1 Timothy 6:10).

How we use our money is no small matter. It goes all the way to the heart of our relationship with God and our lives as disciples of Jesus Christ.

Wisdom is more valuable than money.

The ancient Hebrew sages taught:

Happy are those who find wisdom
    and those who gain understanding.
Her profit is better than silver,
    and her gain better than gold.
                    (Proverbs 3:13-14)

Though multitudes of people around the world suffer the burden of abject poverty and economic injustice, my assumption is that most of the people reading this book do not need more money so much as they need more wisdom in how to manage it. These assumptions lead us directly to John Wesley.

EARN. SAVE. GIVE.

John Wesley (1703–1791) provided practical wisdom for Christians in the use of their money. South African leader Peter Storey wrote, "By far the most important element of Wesley's engagement with social issues was his development of a Gospel-shaped behaviour toward money and riches that was predicated on his commitment to the poor."[5]

Wesley affirmed the use of money as "an excellent branch of Christian wisdom" that was "a subject largely spoken of, after their manner, by men of the world; but not sufficiently considered by those whom God hath chosen out of the world."[6]

In his classic sermon, "The Use of Money," Wesley defined some basic practices regarding money that are just as practical today as they were when he first taught them. "Having, First, gained all you can, and, Secondly saved all you can, Then 'give all you can.' "[7]

In modern language, Wesley's rules for money were simple: Earn all you can. Save all you can. Give all you can.

The purpose of this book and program is to engage disciples of Jesus Christ in a four-week process of study, personal reflection, group sharing, and practical action that will enable them to apply Wesley's wisdom to the way they earn, save, and give.

This book provides a basis for that experience by engaging participants in interpreting Wesley's rules on the use of money for our time. The book includes biblical reflection based largely on the Old Testament Book of Proverbs, along with practical application from a wide variety of personal experiences.

The companion DVD brings the study to life through conversations with contemporary disciples who demonstrate the wisdom of Wesley's rules in their own experience.

The Leader Guide provides practical directions for small-group leaders to engage participants in their own reflection and action. The Youth Study Book and Children's Leader Guide are designed to enable children and youth to begin growing in their understanding of the use of money at their level of spiritual formation.

The Devotional Readings for Home describes, over a four-week period, Wesley's simple rules for money, presents five daily devotions per week to help readers meditate about stewardship, and suggests followup activities for individuals and families to translate their devotions into action.

The Program Guide on Flash Drive gives congregational leaders specific guidance in planning and implementing the program. It includes sermon starters, sample announcements, letters, e-mail and Twitter text, plus graphics for presentation slides, posters, and flyers. In addition, I've included three short mentoring videos for use by pastors and church leaders as they plan their program.

The goal of the program—as well as the goal of Wesley's teachings on money—is not fund-raising to support the ministries of the church, although that is a by-product of spiritual growth in financial stewardship. The goal is to enable disciples of Jesus Christ to discover wisdom that will guide them in using their money, so they may continue to grow into the likeness of Jesus Christ. They will receive practical guidance for the journey toward what Wesley called "the farther end" of generous life that is formed in the likeness of God's extravagant generosity.[8]

I write as the grateful son of parents who taught us the meaning of financial stewardship and demonstrated it in the way they lived. This program also grows out of my experience with faithful disciples in the congregations I have served in Tampa, Orlando, Crescent City, and DeLand, Florida. They taught me more about the use of money than I was ever able to teach them. Most of all, I give thanks for my wife, Martha, whose faithful stewardship and good judgment in the use of money continue to frame the way we earn, save, and give.

We offer this resource in the spirit of a prayer written by Charles Wesley, John Wesley's brother and partner in ministry:

Come, wisdom, power, and grace divine;
Come, Jesus, in thy name to join
A happy, chosen band;
Who fain would prove thine utmost will,
And all thy righteous laws fulfil,
In love's benign command.

Supply what every member wants;
To found the fellowship of saints,
Thy Spirit, Lord, supply;
So shall we all thy love receive,
Together to thy glory live,
And to thy glory die.[9]

WE DON'T NEED MORE MONEY; WE NEED WISDOM

Happy are those who find wisdom
and those who gain understanding.
Her profit is better than silver,
and her gain better than gold.
(Proverbs 3:13-14)

Stanley Johnson was a lot like many of us. A character in a classic Lending Tree television commercial, Stanley flashed a self-satisfied smile as he showed us his four-bedroom home in a great neighborhood, his swimming pool, and his new car. He beamed with pride as he told us he was a member of the local golf club.

Turning steaks on the grill, he asked, "How do I do it?" Still smiling, he confided, "I'm in debt up to my eyeballs. I can barely pay my finance charges." Then, looking directly into the camera, he pleaded, "Somebody help me."[1]

We may not be in as much of a financial mess as Stanley was, but most of us some of the time, and some of us most of the time, need help in managing our money. How we earn it, save it, spend it, and give it is a persistent challenge for every follower of Christ.

Stanley Johnson's commercial was for a lending company, but Stanley didn't really need more money. What he needed was wisdom. When it comes to dealing with money, that's what all of us need. The good news is that wisdom can be found in Scripture and in the Wesleyan tradition.

Information about how to manage our money is easy to find. It is readily available from a multitude of sources, some of which are more helpful and trustworthy than others. Advice about everything from taxes to long-term investments can be acquired in online programs and from financial planners. Stockbrokers, mortgage brokers, and investment bankers are eagerly awaiting our calls. Lawyers and estate planners are standing in line to help us write our wills and plan our legacy. The information we gain from them is a necessary tool for living responsibly with our resources.

As a pastor, I've seen ample evidence of the need for information about finances.

- I'm concerned about young adults who become the prisoners of credit card debt. Listening to their stories has convinced me that credit card debt is nothing less than the demonic power of institutionalized greed taking control of their lives.

- I've counseled with couples who bring nearly insurmountable levels of debt into their marriages because they never learned how to design a budget or balance a checkbook.
- I've watched seminary graduates enter the pastorate—not usually considered a high-income career—with educational loans that will be a long-term burden on their ministries and families.
- I'm surprised by the number of colleagues who retire without adequate planning for financial stability.
- I'm curious about faithful church members who have never prepared a will or an estate plan.

All these concerns and others like them challenge us to use the best information we can about the most effective ways to manage our money.

But for followers of Christ, the issue digs deeper and reaches further than simply gathering information. The Bible teaches that how we relate to our money goes to the heart of our relationship with God.

I sometimes wish Jesus hadn't said, "Where your treasure is, there your heart will be also" (Matthew 6:21). I'd be more comfortable if he had said, "Where your heart is, there your treasure will be also." But he said what he meant and he meant what he said. Our attitudes toward money and the priority we place on our possessions are matters of the heart; they go to the core of our identity. Because of the soul-level importance of our relationship with money, we need more than information. We need wisdom.

WHERE WISDOM IS FOUND

"Where shall wisdom be found?
And where is the place of understanding?"
(Job 28:12 NRSV)

The search for wisdom draws us with magnetic force to the Old Testament Book of Proverbs. The book opens with this promise:

There's something here also for
seasoned men and women,
    still a thing or two for the experienced to learn—
Fresh wisdom to probe and penetrate,
    the rhymes and reasons of wise men and women.
(Proverbs 1:5-6 *The Message*)

The Hebrew word for *wisdom* appears 318 times in the Old Testament with over half of these in Proverbs, Job, and Ecclesiastes.[2] The sages of ancient Israel knew that wisdom is more than the accumulation of information or knowledge, as important as that knowledge is. They understood wisdom to be a gift of God that enables us to know what to do with the knowledge we gather, so we can live faithfully and well in our relationships with God and each other.

Old Testament scholar Ellen Davis observes that the biblical writers had no interest in "knowledge that is abstracted from goodness."[3] Davis also acknowledges that few of us would include Proverbs on our "shortlist of favorite spiritual books." She says our neglect of the Proverbs is often because they are "so down-to-earth, so ordinary."[4]

I'll confess that across four decades of pastoral ministry, I never invested much homiletical horsepower in preaching on them. If you go to Proverbs looking for soul-stretching theological insights or dramatic narratives about the way God intersects our human existence, you'll be sorely disappointed. That's also the reason this collection of pithy aphorisms, brief teachings, and wise sayings barely made it into the canon of Scripture. Davis calls it "a book for unexceptional people trying to live wisely and faithfully in the generally undramatic circumstances of daily life."[5]

But perhaps the earthy ordinariness of the Proverbs is their greatest gift to us, particularly in dealing with something as down-to-earth as our money. In their simplicity, the Proverbs provide practical wisdom for making our way through the mundane places and ordinary relationships of life. We could call them the inspired version of *Poor Richard's Almanack*, which along with weather forecasts and household hints included Benjamin Franklin's homey aphorisms and simple proverbs, many of which focused on work, thrift, and frugality.

The Hebrew word *mashal* literally means "a saying" that is often based on comparison or contrast.[6] Intentionally succinct and designed for oral instruction, the Proverbs are easily memorized and highly transportable. They don't require intensive theological analysis or interpretation. You don't need a preacher or theologian to unpack the historical context or explain what the writers intended. They simply say what they mean and mean what they say. Period. To quote another classic commercial, what you see is what you get.

The Proverbs also have been described as "the encoding of a lived experience."[7] Ellen Davis points out that "it takes a tradition, the accumulated experience and insight of a people, to produce wisdom."[8]

The Hebrew Proverbs wear well because they were formed over generations in the rough and tumble of daily lives. They emerged from, were tested in, and were confirmed by ordinary human experience. Picture the wise old patriarch who has experienced just about everything life could throw at him, sitting beside a campfire or riding a camel through the desert, telling the next generation what he has learned from generations before him. It's wisdom born out of experience.

After being passed on orally for generations, the Proverbs were gathered by Hebrew editors who announced their purpose in the opening verses:

> Their purpose is to teach wisdom and discipline,
> > to help one understand wise sayings.
> They provide insightful instruction,
> > which is righteous, just, and full of integrity.
> They make the naive mature,
> > the young knowledgeable and discreet.
>
> (Proverbs 1:2-4)

Eugene Peterson paraphrased that purpose statement to say that the Proverbs were "written down so we'll know how to live well and right, / to understand what life means and where it's going; . . . / To teach the inexperienced the ropes / and give our young people a grasp on reality" (Proverbs 1:2-4, *The Message*).

As we'll see below, a few key themes unlock the wisdom of Proverbs for us.

WISDOM BEGINS WITH GOD

Wisdom begins with the fear of the LORD,
> but fools despise wisdom and instruction.
> > (Proverbs 1:7)

The beginning of wisdom is the fear of the LORD;
> the knowledge of the holy one
> is understanding. (9:10)

The LORD gives wisdom;
> from his mouth come knowledge
> and understanding. (2:6)

With ruthless clarity, the Proverbs undermine one of the most pervasive assumptions of our post-Enlightenment, scientifically minded culture. Our culture has conditioned us to believe that human beings are the source of knowledge and that wisdom comes from the accumulation of information, in much the same way that wealth comes from the accumulation of money and property. As a result, we assume that the more we know, the wiser we are.

But the Hebrew sages believed that wisdom does not begin with us. It doesn't grow out of our human capacity for learning or our ability to gather information. They were convinced that true wisdom is not something we make up on our own; it is a unique gift growing out of our relationship with God.

This is not to suggest that biblical wisdom is contrary to empirical or academic knowledge, or that the Bible contains answers to questions that are better addressed by science. For example, the creation narratives in Genesis were not intended to answer questions about the origin or evolution of the universe, but to celebrate the One who created it and to give us wisdom about how to live together in it. Similarly, the healing stories in the Gospels are not a substitute for medical care. In fact, the Proverbs tend to confirm the practical lessons for living that grow out of experientially proven truth about our world.

The wisdom that guides us into personal and spiritual maturity is not of our own making. It goes beyond the accumulation of knowledge and instead guides us to use that knowledge in ways that are just, good, and in harmony with God's life-giving purpose.

The painful evidence of history is that knowledge without wisdom can as easily be used for destructive ends as for constructive ones. How else can we account for the fact that when Hitler came to power,

Germany was one of the most intellectually, scientifically, and theologically advanced nations in the world? It was not a question of intellectual knowledge, but of the ends for which that knowledge would be used. It was not a lack of information, but a lack of spiritual, moral, and ethical wisdom that ultimately led to the horror of Auschwitz.

The Bible makes it clear that the wisdom to use information is not inherent in humans but is directly related to our relationship with God. Jesus pointed his disciples in that direction when he said, "Desire first and foremost God's kingdom and God's righteousness, and all these things will be given to you as well" (Matthew 6:33).

Perhaps the most disturbing word in Proverbs is *fear*. We are told, "The beginning of wisdom is the fear of the LORD" (9:10). I'd be happier if the proverb said that the beginning of wisdom is the *love* of the Lord, but the word is *fear*.

The Hebrew word *yare*, or *fear*, appears 370 times in the Old Testament (New American Standard Bible).[9] Some of the newer translations try to soften the language by using the word *reverence*, and that's a very good word. In fact, the meaning of *yare* includes the sense of awe, wonder, and amazement conveyed by *reverence*. We could use more reverence in a time when some forms of Christian worship have become as casual as a coffee shop and our talk about God has become downright chummy, as if God were the friendly neighbor next door who is always ready to help us out when we get in trouble. A strong dose of reverence could cure some of the shallow spirituality that bubbles up around us like sparking water.

But *reverence* doesn't carry the gut-level jolt of *fear*, or the further meanings of *terror* or *dread* that the Hebrew word also conveys.[10] Healthy, appropriate fear wakes us up. It surprises us. It opens our eyes. It sends adrenaline surging through our body and makes our heart pump faster. It shakes us out of our comfortable complacency. It calls for a response. Fear makes things happen.

Throughout Scripture, when imperfect, finite human beings encounter the perfect, infinite presence of God, their most appropriate response is fear. It is no small thing that when angels show up in Scripture, their first words are almost always "Do not be afraid."

There is wisdom that is only gained through an experience of fear; not neurotic, self-absorbed, irrational fear, but fear that acknowledges the magnitude of the issues we face. It's fear that stands in awestricken amazement before that which is beyond our power to manage, explain, or control. It's the kind of fear that leads us to humility. Ellen Davis describes it as "the deeply sane recognition that we are not God."[11]

All of which is to say that we find wisdom through humility. Humility undermines our self-assured arrogance and pride. It challenges the assumption that the answers to all our questions are within ourselves. It requires an openness to discover something we would not otherwise comprehend.

Fear of the Lord is the starting point, because it calls for humble trust in the God who is the source of wisdom and the giver of every good gift (Proverbs 2:6; James 1:17). It challenges us to

Trust in the LORD with all your heart;
   don't rely on your own intelligence.
Know him in all your paths,
   and he will keep your ways straight.
                    (Proverbs 3:5-6)

WISDOM IS PASSED ON TO THE NEXT GENERATION

Uncle Frank was the wise sage in our extended family. Everyone who knew him recognized a genuine goodness in the way he lived his life. He taught American history in a small, country high school for nearly five decades. Although he never became financially wealthy, his life was filled with the wealth of wisdom that grows out of a life lived with clear priorities on the things that matter most. The multiple generations of students who were in his classes not only gathered knowledge; they found wisdom. He gave the same gift to his children and grandchildren and to a wide circle of cousins and their children. These family members looked forward to sitting on the back porch and experiencing the strength of his laughter and the wisdom born out of his long, faithful, and sometimes difficult life.

I hear Uncle Frank's voice in the persistent repetition of phrases such as these in Proverbs:

Listen, my son, to your father's instruction;
    don't neglect your mother's teaching. (1:8)

Now children, listen to me,
    and don't deviate from the
    words of my mouth. (5:7)

Now children, listen to me:
    Happy are those who keep to my ways! (8:32)

If, my child, you stop listening to discipline,
    you will wander away from words
    of knowledge. (19:27)

Listen, my child, and be wise! (23:19)

There is a relational quality to wisdom that is deeper than knowledge and reaches beyond the accumulation of information. Even as wisdom grows out of our relationship with God, it is passed on through our relationships with others.

The writer of Psalm 78 also affirmed the way wisdom is passed on through the generations:

> Listen, my people, to my teaching;
>> tilt your ears toward the words of my mouth.
> I will open my mouth with a proverb.
>> I'll declare riddles from days long gone—
>>> ones that we've heard and learned about,
>>> ones that our ancestors told us.
> We won't hide them from their descendants;
>> we'll tell the next generation
>> all about the praise due the
>> Lord and his strength—
>> the wondrous works God has done.
> He established a law for Jacob
>> and set up Instruction for Israel,
>>> ordering our ancestors
>>> to teach them to their children.
> This is so that the next generation
>> and children not yet born will know these things,
>>> and so they can rise up and tell their children
>> to put their hope in God... (Psalm 78:1-7)

Ideally this kind of life wisdom is passed on through the family the way Timothy received the gift of faith from his mother and grandmother (2 Timothy 1:5). I'm one of those fortunate people whose basic wisdom about life was nurtured in a family that formed its values around a central commitment to Christ.

More specifically, I received financial wisdom from my parents. They demonstrated how to use debt responsibly and how to live within our means. When I began delivering *The Pittsburgh Press* on my bicycle, they took me to the bank and helped me set up a checking account and a savings account. They showed me how to balance a checkbook. They taught me to tithe by returning the first 10 percent of my income to the God who had given it to me. I learned wisdom about the use of money by what they taught and by how they lived.

Unfortunately, that is not the case in every human family. In cases where it's not true, it becomes the responsibility of the faith community to teach the next generation. That's why *Earn. Save. Give.* includes resources for children and youth. Passing financial wisdom to future generations is one of the best gifts we can give.

Wisdom Is Better Than Wealth

The Hebrew sages were clear that, given the choice between wisdom and wealth, we should always choose wisdom.

Happy are those who find wisdom
and those who gain understanding.
Her profit is better than silver,
and her gain better than gold.
Her value exceeds pearls;
all you desire can't compare with her.
In her right hand is a long life;
in her left are wealth and honor.
(Proverbs 3:13-16)

These early sages were convinced that some of the most important choices we make are not between good or evil but between what is wise and what is foolish. The words *wise* and *wisdom* appear 111 times in the Proverbs; the words *fool* and *foolish* appear 77 times (NRSV).[12]

Jesus drew on this wisdom tradition in painting the contrast between wise and foolish servants (Matthew 24:45-51), bridesmaids (Matthew 25:1-13), and builders (Matthew 7:24-27). He told the story of a rich man whose fields produced more than his barns could contain. Instead of sharing his wealth, the man hoarded it by building larger barns and told himself, "Take it easy! Eat, drink, and enjoy yourself." The culture in which we live would call him wise. But God said, "Fool, tonight you will die. Now who will get the things you have prepared for yourself?" Jesus added the punch line to the story: "This is the way it will be for those who hoard things for themselves and aren't rich toward God" (Luke 12:19-21). Knowing the difference calls for wisdom.

The Book of Proverbs concludes with the powerful description of a strong, capable woman (Proverbs 31:10-31) whose "mouth is full of wisdom" (31:26). Her family celebrates the wisdom they have received from her.

> Her children bless her;
>> her husband praises her:
>> "Many women act competently,
>> but you surpass them all!"
> Charm is deceptive and beauty fleeting,
>> but a woman who fears
>> the LORD is to be praised.
> Let her share in the results of her work;
>> let her deeds praise her in the
>> city gates. (31:28-31)

Wisdom Leads to Life

Don't consider yourself wise.
    Fear the LORD and turn away from evil.
Then your body will be healthy
    and your bones strengthened.
Honor the LORD with your wealth
    and with the first of all your crops.
Then your barns will be filled with plenty,
    and your vats will burst with wine.
                    (Proverbs 3:7-10)

Those words could be a perfect text for the "prosperity gospel" preachers who declare that God intends for us to be rich. The size of their congregations, the ratings of their television programs, and the place their books hold on the best-seller lists confirm that there is always a market for their emotional manipulation and dubious theology.

And yet, the kernel of biblical truth that they effectively distort is that the Bible does have positive things to say about the results of wise living that are just as true today as when the Proverbs were written.

- It's wise to use our talents and the opportunities that come our way to earn an honest income. It's foolish to bury our talents and never find

productive ways to use them. (Matthew 25:
26-30)

- It's wise to use our money well by living within
  our means. It's foolish to be like the prodigal
  son who "wasted his wealth through extravagant living." (Luke 15:13)
- It's wise to manage our money in order to
  become debt-free. It's foolish to be consumed
  by unnecessary and unmanageable debt.
  (Proverbs 11:15)

Wise living may not insure that we will be rich,
but it always leads to a healthy, prosperous, abundant
life. It's the deeper wisdom Paul expressed when he
wrote:

> I know the experience of being in need and
> of having more than enough; I have learned
> the secret to being content in any and every
> circumstance, whether full or hungry or whether
> having plenty or being poor. I can endure all
> these things through the power of the one who
> gives me strength. (Philippians 4:12-13)

Biblical wisdom on the use of money is centered
in helping faithful people order their financial lives
around their commitment to Christ so that they can
live well in every area of their lives. All of which

35

brings us to John Wesley and his words of wisdom about money.

Wisdom from Wesley

The eighteenth century was a time of major economic and social change in England. The economic inequality between the comfortable, affluent aristocracy and the beleaguered, poverty-stricken lower classes was growing larger and more tenuous.

The first Methodists came on the scene with a life-giving proclamation of the gospel that offered hope for transformation in every area of human experience. Some historians say that the Methodist revival saved England from the kind of violent revolution that swept across Western Europe.[13] The personal and spiritual disciplines that John Wesley practiced and taught enabled people in the lower classes to become more responsible, better educated, and more prosperous. Soon Wesley faced the unexpected predicament of Methodist people accumulating wealth, wearing fine clothing, and building more attractive homes and preaching houses.

Wesley responded to this change of economic circumstances in his classic sermon, "The Use of Money." He used the defining word from the Proverbs when he declared that "the right use of money" is "an excellent branch of Christian *wisdom*" (italics added). In fact, the word *wisdom* appears seven times in this sermon. He acknowledged that money was "a subject largely spoken of . . . by men of the world; but not sufficiently considered by those whom God hath chosen out of the world."[14]

We could say the same thing about many congregations today in which the only time money is mentioned is during an annual pledge drive to support the church budget. But Wesley's concern in the sermon was not to raise money for the Methodist movement; his purpose was to equip Methodists to manage and use their money in the most faithful and effective ways. In this sermon, he set out the essential themes that he continued to proclaim in multiple sermons that were intended to provide wisdom on both the spiritual and practical aspects of managing money.

Wesley's text was Jesus' strange command to "make to yourselves friends of the mammon of unrighteousness" (Luke 16:9 KJV). It's an odd statement, taken from an even more bizarre story of a dishonest manager who, when confronted with a financial crisis, was smart enough to look out for his own welfare (Luke 16:1–9). Here's the way Eugene Peterson paraphrased the punch line of the parable.

"Now here's a surprise: The master praised the crooked manager! And why? Because he knew how to look after himself. Streetwise people are smarter in this regard than law-abiding citizens. They are on constant alert, looking for angles, surviving by their wits. I want you to be smart in the same way—but for what is *right*—using every adversity to stimulate you to creative survival, to concentrate your attention on the bare essentials, so you'll live, really live, and not complacently just get by on good behavior." (Luke 16:8-9 *The Message*)

The parable is followed by Jesus' application of the story to the relationship between our faith and our finances.

"If you're honest in small things,
    you'll be honest in big things;
If you're a crook in small things,
    you'll be a crook in big things.
If you're not honest in small jobs,
    who will put you in charge of the store?
No worker can serve two bosses:
    He'll either hate the first and love the second
Or adore the first and despise the second.
    You can't serve both God and the Bank."
(Luke 16:10-13 *The Message)*

The story turns our expectations inside out. The crook becomes the hero because of the way he managed his money. And that's precisely the kind of twist that Wesley built into his sermon.

Mr. Wesley began by countering the assumption that money is "the grand corrupter of the world, the bane of virtue, the pest of human society." He called this kind of negative talk about money "an empty rant." Referencing Paul's words to Timothy, he pointed out that " 'the love of money . . . is the root of all evil;' but not the thing itself. The fault does not lie in the money, but in them that use it." Wesley went on to celebrate money as "an excellent gift of God, answering the noblest ends."[15]

It would be difficult to find a nobler vision for the use of money than the one Wesley gives:

In the hands of his children, it is food for the hungry, drink for the thirsty, raiment for the naked. . . . By it we may supply the place of an husband to the widow, and of a father to the fatherless; we may be a defence for the oppressed, a means of health to the sick, of ease to them that are in pain. It may be as eyes to the blind, as feet to the lame; yea, a lifter up from the gates of death![16]

From that starting point, Mr. Wesley outlined what he called "three plain rules" on the use of money. They are as simple, clear, and memorable as any of the Old Testament proverbs:

- Gain all you can.
- Save all you can.
- Give all you can.

For this study, we have replaced the word *gain* with *earn*, to make Wesley's rules more directly applicable to our times.

"The Use of Money" laid out a description of what it means to live by those rules, and he reaffirmed them in a number of his other sermons. Two-and-a-half centuries later, Wesley's rules continue to provide practical and positive wisdom for discovering a faithful, biblical, and hopeful approach to our financial lives. Like the Proverbs, they lay out time-tested, experience-proven disciplines that if practiced over time can lead to a healthy relationship between our faith and our finances.

In the weeks ahead, we will explore Wesley's guidance on money in the context of the wisdom in the Proverbs and the words and witness of the New Testament. Our purpose is to engage followers of Christ in a process of Bible study, personal reflection, prayer, and action that will lead to practical, biblical, and Christ-centered wisdom about how we use our money.

Stanley Johnson could have been speaking for any of us when he pleaded, "Somebody help me." What he needed was wisdom. That's exactly what Mr. Wesley wanted to provide. Our expectation is that as we reclaim this part of our Wesleyan spiritual heritage, we will discover the kind of wisdom that will help us grow in our own discipleship and engage with others in making a difference in our congregations and communities.

The good news is that we do not enter into this study alone. We join with generations of Christians before us, Methodist and otherwise, who have proven the wisdom of Wesley's words, and we begin by claiming the promise that comes to us from the Epistle of James:

Anyone who needs wisdom should ask God,
whose very nature is to give to everyone without
a second thought, without keeping score. Wisdom
will certainly be given to those who ask.

(James 1:5)

—2—

Earn All You Can

Laziness brings poverty;
hard work makes one rich.
(Proverbs 10:4)

When was the last time you were surprised by what the preacher had to say?

I'll never forget an old guy in the first congregation I served who had been in the church all his life. He sat in the back row and went to sleep during the sermon every Sunday morning. One day on the way out of worship he explained his behavior. "Well, Preacher," he said, "I listen to the first part of your sermon and when I know I can trust what you're going to say, I figure I can get in a good nap." It became my personal challenge to surprise that guy with something he didn't expect just to keep him awake.

I suspect that many of John Wesley's most faithful followers were a lot like those of us who listen to sermons every Sunday morning. We may not go to sleep,

but once we hear the Scripture and listen to the opening illustration, we often assume that we know what
the preacher is going to say. The challenge for the
preacher is to surprise us with something we didn't
expect to hear.

John Wesley's sermon "The Use of Money"
must have come as a surprise to some of the early
Methodists. It still has the power to take us by surprise.

The first surprise might have been Mr. Wesley's
choice for the Scripture reading—the disturbing parable of the dishonest servant (Luke 16:1-13). In the
story, Jesus clearly intended to surprise the hearers. If
something about his story doesn't surprise or offend
us, we probably haven't really heard it.

Wesley began by pointing out that Jesus told the
story "to his disciples" (16:1). It's a message to the
"insiders," a word of guidance for people who already
are followers of Christ. It's a story for "church folks"
like most of us. From the beginning, this suggests
that people who have accepted the invitation to be
disciples of Jesus Christ see the world differently
than others. They approach every decision—including decisions about money—from a different set of
assumptions. Their starting point is their commitment
to a life in which they love God and love others.

The surprise in Jesus' story is the way the master
praised the crooked manager for being smart enough

to cook the books so that he would be taken care of in the future.

> "The master commended the dishonest manager because he acted cleverly. People who belong to this world are more clever in dealing with their peers than are people who belong to the light. I tell you, use worldly wealth to make friends for yourselves so that when it's gone, you will be welcomed into the eternal homes." (Luke 16:8-9)

Read that story in most congregations, and I can assure you that someone will be asking, "What on earth is the preacher going to do with a story like that?"

The next surprise came when Wesley contradicted the assumption that wealth and money are inherently evil. It's a safe bet that his first hearers thought of money as "filthy lucre." They had been steeped in the language of the King James Version of the New Testament in which that phrase appears five times, all of them negative: 1 Timothy 3:3, 8; Titus 1:7, 11; 1 Peter 5:2. People of that era would also have been familiar with John Bunyan's book *Pilgrim's Progress*, in which the main character, named Christian, comes to a small hill called "Lucre" in which there was a silver mine. Bunyan wrote:

Some of them had formerly gone that way...
but going too near the brim of the pit, the ground
being deceitful under them, broke, and they were
slain; some also had been maimed there, and could
not, to their dying day, be their own men again.

When Christian came near the mountain of Lucre,
he was tempted to stop and check it out. But he refused
the temptation and said, "Not I . . . I have heard of this
place before now and how many have been slain
there; and besides, that treasure is a snare to those
that seek it; for it hindereth them in their pilgrimage."[1]

Wesley acknowledged the long tradition of "poets,
orators, and philosophers, in almost all ages and
nations, to rail at [money], as the grand corrupter of
the world, the bane of virtue, the pest of human society."[2] That's what his hearers expected him to say.
It's what they would have heard before. Given the
fact that most early Methodists came from the lower
economic classes in British society, they also would
have believed it because of their experiences with the
wealthy upper classes.

It must have come as a surprise, then, to hear their
spiritual leader call money "an excellent gift of God."
Wesley raised the bar on the spiritual importance
of money when he called it "a most compendious
instrument of transacting all manner of business, and

(if we use it according to Christian wisdom) of doing all manner of good."[3]

Wesley declared "the right use of money" to be "an excellent branch of Christian wisdom" that is "not sufficiently considered by those whom God hath chosen out of the world.... Neither do they understand how to employ it to the greatest advantage."[4]

Wesley's critique of Christians who do not know how to manage or use money "to the greatest advantage" could still apply to many faithful people and congregations today. I've known people who believed that wise financial planning was somehow a contradiction of their trust in God. I've known congregations that functioned without wise management of their resources and without adequate methods of financial accountability. Regardless of the sincerity of their faith, sooner or later those individuals and congregations always end up in some kind of financial crisis.

By contrast, I've been grateful for the wise, experienced, and deeply faithful laypersons in every congregation I've served who use their best knowledge and experience with money to guide the church in the wise stewardship of the gifts of God's people. Their financial wisdom is not a contradiction of their faith, but an expression of it.

THE FIRST RULE OF CHRISTIAN WISDOM

Wesley's affirmation of the wise use of money set the stage for what may have been the biggest surprise of all. Wesley declared that it was the "bounden duty" of Christian disciples to practice what he called the "first and great rule of Christian wisdom," namely "Gain [earn] all you can."[5] My guess is they didn't see that one coming.

Jem Lugo, in her high school valedictorian speech, surprised her fellow graduates when she told them, "Get money. You can't do anything without money. Do something with your life where you're able to have a steady, reliable source of income. Gamers, I'm sorry, but farming for gold in World of Warcraft [a video game] is not considered a reliable or socially acceptable source of income."[6] Jem probably would have been surprised to learn that in her own way she was channeling John Wesley. She was offering a word of wisdom from Wesley that still has the power to surprise us.

The first time I preached on Wesley's rules for money, a faithful church member told me he had never heard anything like that from a preacher before. He thought there were only two options for a preacher. One was the questionable "get rich quick" promise of prosperity-gospel preachers. The other was the pretentious piety of preachers who acted as if dealing with money was somehow beneath them and who only timidly pleaded for money for the church because the finance committee required them to do it.

My friend assumed that the only word the Bible had to offer on wealth and money was that it would be easier for a camel to get through the eye of a needle than for a rich person to get into heaven (Matthew 19:24), a text which Wesley later used as the basis of his sermon entitled, "On Riches." As a result, my friend wrestled with an inner tension between his faith in Christ and his ambition to prosper in his work. Like the ancient Hebrew proverbs, this simple, clear, and memorable word from Wesley created a new opportunity for my friend and his wife to discover a more meaningful connection between their work, their money, and their faith.

He wasn't alone. When he shared his thoughts with the members of his covenant group, they all agreed that he was describing what they had experienced, too.

Wesley, having surprised us with his affirmation of the spiritual value of money, went on to define three practical guidelines for the way faithful followers of Jesus can gain or earn all they can.

1. GAIN ALL YOU CAN BY HONEST INDUSTRY. USE ALL POSSIBLE DILIGENCE IN YOUR CALLING.[7]

Don't miss Wesley's use of the word *calling*. Wesley was standing squarely in the center of Protestant tradition by affirming that God's calling or "vocation" is not only for persons who are called to be pastors. All disciples are called to use their gifts in ways that accomplish God's best purpose for their lives and help fulfill God's life-giving purpose in the world.

Two centuries before Wesley, reformer Martin Luther had surprised people by applying the word *vocation* to the work of laity as well as to monks and priests.

The works of monks and priests, however holy and arduous they may be, do not differ one whit in the sight of God from the works of the rustic laborer in the field or the woman going about her household tasks . . . all works are measured before God by faith alone.[8]

Luther's affirmation elevated the value of every person's work. It invited all followers of Christ to listen for God's calling based on their unique abilities, opportunities, and passions. As an example, I can bear witness that my wife's career as an elementary school teacher has always been just as clearly her calling as mine has been to be a pastor.

The same affirmation appears in John Wesley's "Collection of Hymns for The Use of the People Called Methodist" in hymn text by John Ellerton which is sometimes attributed to Charles Wesley :

Yet these [the church] are not the only walls
Wherein thou may'st be sought;
On homeliest work thy blessing falls
In truth and patience wrought.

Thine is the loom, the forge, the mart,
The wealth of land and sea;
The worlds of science and of art,
Revealed and ruled by thee.

Then let us prove our heavenly birth
In all we do and know,
And claim the kingdom of the earth
For thee, and not thy foe.

Work shall be prayer, if all be wrought
As thou wouldst have it done;
And prayer, by thee inspired and taught,
Itself with work be one.[9]

The last funeral service I preached in my final appointment before retirement was for a very successful banker who had grown up in a Methodist family that was so poor that he and his brother, in order to earn a little bit of money, took the job of firing up the coal furnace at their country church on Sunday mornings. He was able to go to college because of a Methodist scholarship that was supposed to be reserved for preministerial students. When he confessed to the bishop that he did not feel called to the ministry, the wise bishop told him to go on to college because God could use him as a layperson just as well as God could use him as a preacher.

That's what he did, and he spent the rest of his life expressing his gratitude for that scholarship. He guided our congregation in building an endowment fund that would provide scholarships for another generation of students. In the funeral sermon, I said that he would have been a lousy preacher, but he became a fine Christian layperson who used his ability to manage money in ways that confirmed the bishop's wisdom and God's calling in his life.

Seeing our work as a calling from God puts the challenge to "earn all you can" in the context of the larger purpose for our work. Wesley's instruction is not merely to earn money for its own sake but to earn it for the higher purpose of fulfilling God's intention for our lives.

Jim Collins discovered the same principle in the secular business world. He found that "visionary companies pursue a cluster of objectives, of which making money is only one—and not necessarily the primary one." His research showed that companies that are successful over time "seek profits, but they're equally guided by . . . core values and sense of purpose beyond just making money." In fact, Collins showed that over the long haul "the visionary companies make more money than the more purely profit-driven comparison companies."[10]

Shark Tank is one of the most popular reality shows on television today. A group of wealthy, highly successful investors—known as "sharks"—interview ordinary people who are attempting to launch a new business or product and who are looking for one or more of the sharks to invest in their product. If one or more of the sharks choose to invest, the entrepreneur comes away with financial capital and a strong partner. If no shark chooses to invest, the entrepreneur leaves empty-handed.

One of the sharks is blatantly and sometimes brutally interested only in making money. He can be downright rude in attacking the weakness in either the presentation or the product. But a couple of the other sharks are not only interested in making a profit, but also in making a difference. They are drawn to the character of the potential partner or the positive difference that this particular business or product will make in the lives of others.

Wesley, because he believed that every person's work can be a calling from God, challenged Christians to "use all possible diligence in your calling."

> Lose no time. If you understand yourself and your relation to God and man, you know you have none to spare. If you understand your particular calling as you ought, you will have no time that hangs upon your hands. Every business will afford some employment sufficient for every day and every hour.... Never leave anything till to-morrow, which you can do to-day. And do it as well as possible. Do not sleep or yawn over it: Put your whole strength to the work. Spare no pains. Let nothing be done by halves, or in a slight and careless manner. Let nothing in your business be left undone if it can be done by labour or patience.[11]

Wisdom from the Proverbs

In advising Christians to earn money with "all possible diligence," Wesley was reflecting the wisdom of the Proverbs in the way they consistently lift up the positive results of hard work in contrast to the negative results of laziness.

There is profit in hard work,
>   but mere talk leads to poverty. (14:23)

Laziness brings on deep sleep;
>   a slacker goes hungry. (19:15)

The lazy don't plow during winter;
>   at harvest they look but find nothing. (20:4)

The lazy don't roast their prey,
>   but hard workers receive precious riches. (12:27)

The lazy have strong desires but receive nothing;
>   the appetite of the diligent is satisfied. (13:4)

To illustrate the point more clearly, the Hebrew sages drew an example from nature.

Go to the ant, you lazy person;
>   observe its ways and grow wise.
The ant has no commander, officer, or ruler.
>   Even so, it gets its food in summer;
>   gathers its provisions at harvest.
How long, lazy person, will you lie down?
>   When will you rise from your sleep?
A little sleep, a little slumber,
>   a little folding of the arms to lie down—
>   and poverty will come on you like a prowler,
>   destitution like a warrior. (Proverbs 6:6-11)

They drove home the point by concluding their collection of wise sayings with the description of the wise woman in Proverbs 31.

> She seeks out wool and flax;
>> she works joyfully with her hands....
> She surveys a field and acquires it;
>> from her own resources, she plants a vineyard.
> She works energetically;
>> her arms are powerful.
> She realizes that her trading is successful;
>> she doesn't put out her lamp at night. . . .
> She makes garments and sells them;
>> she supplies sashes to traders.
>
> (Proverbs 31:13-24)

The wisdom of the Proverbs comes down to us in the New Testament when Jesus commended "the faithful and wise managers" (Luke 12:42-48). His parable of the talents underscored the wise use of the individual gifts that God gives each person (Luke 19:11-27). Paul drew on the same tradition when he called those who had become followers of Christ to "go to work, using their hands to do good so that they will have something to share with whoever is in need" (Ephesians 4:28).

Wesley's words, applicable to all Christians, certainly worked for the people called Methodist. Methodist historian Richard Heitzenrater wrote that "their disciplined efforts to live the Christian life had resulted in a cleaner, more educated, upwardly mobile congregation in many of the Methodist preaching-houses." What Heitzenrater called "the unusual predicament of having Methodists accumulating wealth" prompted Wesley to give his guidance on the use of money.[12]

2. GAIN ALL YOU CAN, BY COMMON SENSE.[13]

Some people bypass the Proverbs because they seem to be nothing more than common sense. But that down-to-earth quality is also part of the wisdom they share, a wisdom gained through common, everyday experience that has been passed on from one generation to another.

The same Proverbs that celebrate the benefits of hard work also include these words of warning and of promise.

The lips of the righteous nourish many people,
  but fools who lack sense will die. (10:21)

Plans fail with no counsel,
  but with many counselors they succeed.(15:22)

Without guidance, a people will fall,
  but there is victory with many counselors (11:14)

Wesley urged his followers, "You should be continually learning, from the experience of others, or from your own experience . . . to do everything you have to do better to-day than you did yesterday."[14]

Jim Collins pointed in the same direction when he wrote, "Good is the enemy of great." He observed, "Few people attain great lives, in large part because it is just so easy to settle for a good life. The vast majority of companies never become great, precisely because the vast majority become quite good—and that is their main problem."[15]

Collins challenged business leaders to create a "culture of discipline," which he defined as "the discipline to do whatever it takes to become the best within carefully selected arenas and then to seek continual improvement from there. It's really just that simple. And it's really just that difficult."[16]

At the centers of great businesses Collins found leaders who practiced "a paradoxical blend of personal humility and professional will . . . self-effacing individuals who displayed the fierce resolve to do whatever needed to be done to make the company great."[17]

Creating a "culture of discipline" is not just for people in the business world. It is true for every one of us as we continue to grow in our spiritual disciplines and in the use of our God-given talents and opportunities. Collins probably would be surprised to learn that over two hundred years ago, John Wesley called his followers to practice the same discipline of constant improvement.

One of the distinguishing marks of wisdom in every area of life is a teachable spirit, including the kind of humility that makes space for learning from others. A wise person is a continuous learner who is always searching for a better way to "do everything you have to do better to-day than you did yesterday."

Foolish people try to do it on their own. They assume that they already have all the knowledge they need. Wise people gain wisdom from others who have been down the road before them.

A Wise Earner

I have a friend whose life bears witness to Wesley's teaching. The only thing my friend inherited from his family was the memory of his mother struggling to keep food on their table and shoes on the children's feet. A sports scholarship enabled him to go to college, after which he put himself through graduate school.

Early in his career, he thought he could make it on his own. As a result, he made several bad financial investments and almost lost everything he had earned. He started over again with enough humility to learn from the wisest people around him. Through Wesleyan diligence in his calling and the wisdom he received from others, he experienced the fulfillment of this promise: "God has the power to provide you with...everything you need always and in everything to provide more than enough for every kind of good work" (2 Corinthians 9:8).

Now approaching retirement, my friend senses that God is calling him to pass on the wisdom he has gained to younger Christians in the workplace. I connected him with several young adults who are searching for wisdom in connecting their faith with their work. He has walked with some of them through the same kind of financial disaster he faced and has helped others avoid making the same mistakes.

Along the way he shares his faith in Christ and his commitment to tithe as the beginning point of a generous lifestyle as his way of fulfilling the command, "Honor the LORD with your wealth / and with the first of all your crops" (Proverbs 3:9). He is demonstrating the way wisdom can be passed on from one generation to another. All it takes is the humility to learn from others and a relentless discipline for constant improvement.

A Foolish Farmer

Jesus told the story of a rich farmer whose land began to produce a bumper crop (Luke 12:13-21). It's a story to which we will return several times in this study. Don't miss the fact that the farmer was already prosperous. He started out with more than he needed and ended up with more than his barns could contain. What would the already prosperous farmer do with his newfound prosperity?

Jesus said the farmer "thought to himself" (12:17 NRSV). In other words, the conversation in the story took place inside the farmer's head. In his sixty-word soliloquy, the farmer used the first person pronoun ten times. He didn't consult a family member, business consultant, tax attorney, or investment advisor. In narcissistic overconfidence, he debated his situation mentally without seeking the wisdom of others and with no regard for God.

In his internal dialogue, the farmer decided to pull down his barns and build bigger ones where he could store all his goods. Then he put up his feet beside the fire and thought, "I'll say to myself, You have stored up plenty of goods, enough for several years. Take it easy! Eat, drink, and enjoy yourself" (12:19, paraphrased).

Gordon Gekko, the iconic character in the movie *Wall Street* who declared that "greed is good," would have called the farmer a success. In today's world, the farmer might have made it to the cover of *Fortune* magazine and become a cable news network personality. Many people would have said he had achieved "the American dream." He had it all!

But God gave a different verdict. God said, "Fool, tonight you will die. Now who will get the things you have prepared for yourself?" (12:20). Jesus' comment on the story was, "Guard yourself against all kinds of greed. After all, one's life isn't determined by one's possessions, even when someone is very wealthy" (12:15).

Proverbs teaches the same lesson:

Such is the end of all who are greedy for gain;
   it takes away the life of its possessors.
                    (Proverbs 1:19 NRSV)

The wisdom in Jesus' story is that it's foolish to live as if we are defined by how much we own, but it's wise to keep a wider perspective on our earning.

It's foolish to think we have all the wisdom we need inside our own experience, but it's wise to be humble enough to gather wisdom from others.

It's foolish to assume that the point of earning money is simply to accumulate more money, but it's wise to use our wealth for a larger purpose than our own satisfaction.

It's foolish to manage our money with no reference to God, but it's wise to earn all we can through diligence to our calling.

This brings us to the third wise word from Wesley.

3. GAIN ALL YOU CAN WITHOUT PAYING MORE FOR IT THAN IT IS WORTH.[18]

Wesley's instruction to "gain [earn] all you can" might sound familiar to those of us who have been conditioned by the mindset of an upwardly mobile, high-achieving, success-driven, consumer-oriented culture. But when we slow down in our race for success long enough to think about it, we know that in that culture, earning all you can becomes a very complicated deal. There is both a good side and a shadow side to this principle.

That's why Wesley challenged us to earn all we can without paying too great a price for it. He spelled out this third principle in specific terms that are just as applicable to us today as they were to the first people who heard them.

Earn all you can, but not at the expense of your health.[19]

Wesley warns us not to "begin or continue in any business which necessarily deprives us of proper seasons for food and sleep."[20] Similarly, the Hebrew sages taught:

> Don't wear yourself out trying to get rich;
>   be smart enough to stop. (Proverbs 23:4)

That's a warning that could surprise and disturb just about all of us! While the danger of laziness as described in the Proverbs is always present, the more present danger in our time is probably the temptation to overwork, driven by compulsive consumerism and relentless greed.

The biblical answer is the Sabbath, *shabbath* "a day of rest" from *shabath* meaning "to cease to do to" or "to rest."[21] The first creation story in Genesis describes the God who did the work of creation but also rested on the seventh day, thereby planting the rhythm of work and rest into the created order. We even find this principle in the soil, which after a productive season of growth needs a "fallow" season to be replenished.

Old Testament scholar Walter Brueggemann argues that honoring the Sabbath is not about simply keeping "blue laws" but about discovering a new way of living that breaks the cycle of anxious acquisition and competition and opens us to new ways of living every day of the week. He calls the discipline of Sabbath an "act of . . . resistance . . . because it is a visible insistence that our lives are not defined by the production and consumption of commodity goods."

Brueggemann lifts up Sabbath as "an alternative to the demanding, chattering, pervasive presence of advertising and its great liturgical claim of professional sports that devour all our 'rest time.' "[22]

Developing a healthy rhythm of work and rest creates a space in which we can experience the presence of the One who said, "Come to me, all you who are struggling hard and carrying heavy loads, and I will give you rest. Put on my yoke, and learn from me. I'm gentle and humble. And you will find rest for yourselves" (Matthew 11:28-29). In the long run, a balanced life is more productive than a life driven by endless work.

Earn all you can, but not at the expense of your soul.[23]

Wesley said, "We must preserve, at all events, the spirit of [a] healthful mind" by not participating in any "sinful trade." He defined "sinful trade" as anything "contrary to the law of God, or of our country," which in Wesley's case included paying "customs" (taxes) to the king. He went on to name any kind of work that "is not consistent with a good conscience."[24] The Proverbs share the same wisdom.

These are the ways of all who seek unjust gain;
    it costs them their lives. (1:19)

The wages of the righteous lead to life;
    the earnings of the wicked lead to sin. (10:16)

I was both inspired and challenged by a parishioner whose job involved providing cable television service to hotels. He came to me as his pastor to discuss the internal conflict he was experiencing when the company he worked for added pornographic movies to their hotel room options. He had experienced the destructive power of pornography in his own life, and as a follower of Christ he was trying to deal with his conscience and continue in his work. At great risk to his own financial security he handed in his resignation, trusting that God would open a new work opportunity for him. He may not have earned as much money in his new job, but he saved his own soul.

Earn all you can, but not at the expense of your neighbor.[25]

At the center of both the gospel and Wesley's theology are the first "great commandment" to love God and the second commandment to love our neighbor. Wesley said that obedience to the second commandment prevents us from doing injury to our neighbor in "substance" (anything that unfairly affects another's economic stability), "body" (anything that injures the neighbor's health), or "soul" (anything that contributes to another person's sin).

Wesley would have been familiar with the writings of John Donne (1572–1631), who is remembered for saying that we are not islands to ourselves but are all part of the main; we are intrinsically connected to one another. Because of this principle, the way we earn our money has a direct impact on the lives of others. We cannot be faithful followers of Jesus Christ if we earn all we can by doing harm to our neighbors.

Preaching at the Riverside Church in New York City in 1983, William Sloane Coffin pointed to "the Biblical truth which insists that there are poor people *because* there are rich people; that the rich, not the poor, are the problem." He spoke of those "who have poverty imposed upon them by an ideology that says, 'What's good for the rich is best for the poor.' "[26]

Coffin's words take on more complex meaning today when we realize they apply not only to the neighbor next door but also to neighbors around the world. My friends in South Africa are quick to remind me that when the US economy gets a cold, the South African economy comes down with pneumonia. It's a fact of life and death that overconsumption by the richest people in the world is stealing resources from the poorest.

President Dwight D. Eisenhower was speaking of that same responsibility when he warned:

Every gun that is made, every warship launched, every rocket fired signifies, in the final sense, a theft from those who hunger and are not fed, those who are cold and not clothed. This world in arms is not spending money alone. It is spending the sweat of its laborers, the genius of its scientists, the hopes of its children.... This is not a way of life at all, in any true sense. Under the cloud of threatening war, it is humanity hanging from a cross of iron.[27]

We are bound together intricately in the global economy and cannot be faithful to Christ if we gain all we can by doing damage to our neighbors, who- ever and wherever they are.

Earn all you can in ways that honor God.

In his sermon "The Good Steward," Wesley said, "We are not at liberty to use what he has lodged in our hands as we please, but as he pleases, who alone is the possessor of heaven and earth."[28]

In his sermon "The More Excellent Way," Wesley described the way Christians, "after using some prayer," should "apply themselves to the business of their calling." He declared that "it is impossible that an idle man can be a good man,—sloth being incon- sistent with religion." But he followed that affirma- tion with a deeper question: "For what end do you undertake and follow your worldly business?"[29]

Wesley acknowledged that providing for our own basic needs and those of our family is "a good answer as far as it goes; but it does not go far enough....A Christian may go abundantly farther." He said that the goal of labor "is to please God...to do the will of God on earth as angels do in heaven....Is not this 'a more excellent way'?"[30] Wesley went on to challenge his followers to combine their work and their piety.

> In what *manner* do you transact your worldly business? I trust, with diligence, whatever your hand findeth to do, doing it with all our might; in justice, rendering to all their due, in every circumstance of life; yea, and in mercy, doing unto every man what you would he should do unto you. This is well: But a Christian is called to go still farther,—to add piety to justice; to intermix prayer, especially the prayer of the heart, with all the labour of his hands. Without this all his diligence and justice only show him to be an honest Heathen.[31]

Finally, Wesley called his followers to do their work in the spirit of Christ. "If you act in the Spirit of Christ you carry the end you at first proposed through all your work from first to last...continually aiming, not at ease, pleasure, or riches...but merely at the glory of God. Now can anyone deny that this is the most excellent way of pursuing worldly business?"[32]

One of the early Methodist hymnals includes a section titled "For Believers, Working." In a similar spirit, a Charles Wesley hymn expresses in prayer the spiritual center of earning all that we can.

> Summoned my labour to renew,
> And glad to act my part,
> Lord, in thy name my work I do,
> And with a single heart.

> End of my every action thou,
> In all things thee I see:
> Accept my hallowed labour now,
> I do it unto thee.[33]

—3—

SAVE ALL YOU CAN

Riches gotten quickly will dwindle,
  but those who acquire them gradually
    become wealthy.
                                        (Proverbs 13:11)

Having earned all we can, we move to Wesley's "second rule of Christian prudence," to save all we can. It's a principle that is simple to state and difficult to do, in large part because it goes against the grain of the culture in which we live.

One of my pastoral mentors liked to say that no one wants to begin where we are; we'd like to begin where we'd be if we had started when we should have. The good news about saving is that it is never too late to begin.

Let's begin this week with two powerfully contrasting stories that invite us to consider the foolishness of hoarding and the wisdom of saving.

[handwritten in margin: The best time to plant a tree is 20 years ago. The second best time is today]

THE FOOLISHNESS OF HOARDING

Homer and Langley Collyer were teenagers in 1909 when their family moved into the three-story brownstone on Fifth Avenue in Harlem, New York City. After they received university educations, their parents moved out of the house and the brothers moved back in. They never left. That's where they died in 1947. They were discovered when an anonymous call to the police reported the smell of a dead body coming from the house. When the police arrived, they were unable to get through the front door because of the mountains of junk piled behind it.

They climbed in through a second-story window and found Homer, who was blind and deaf, slumped over in his chair. He had been dead for several days. Langley was nowhere to be found. Three weeks later they discovered his rotting corpse, crushed under hundreds of boxes, the victim of one of the booby-traps he had set to protect their possessions from intruders he had imagined were trying to break in and steal their stuff.

The entire house was packed from wall to wall and floor to ceiling with bundles, boxes, and piles that included everything from a wine press to a baby carriage. City crews eventually removed more than 130 tons of junk from the house, including decades of old newspapers, broken-down furniture, the chassis of a Model T, fourteen pianos, two organs, and more than 25,000 books. The house was in such disrepair that it had to be torn down.

For decades afterward, New York City firefighters used the term "Collyer's Mansion" to refer to a house that was so full of trash and debris that it became a danger to the occupants, their neighbors, and emergency responders. A small park now marks the spot where their house once stood, a monument to what the Proverbs might have called the destructive foolishness of hoarding.

Homer and Langley were an extreme case. They were suffering from paranoia and a mental disorder we now know as "disposophobia," the fear of throwing away possessions that have little or no real value. Hoarding has even become the theme for reality television shows. But the Collyer brothers' story is just the kind of story Jesus might have told.

Jesus never hesitated to use bold contrasts, visual hyperbole, and shocking exaggeration to demonstrate the dramatic difference between life in the kingdom of God, lived under the reign and rule of God's love revealed in Jesus and life in the kingdoms of this world, lived under the values and assumptions of the world around us. Jesus' parables sometimes create an internal tension that forces us to consider what are described as mutually exclusive alternatives.

That's what Jesus was doing in the Sermon on the Mount when he spoke about our relationship with God and wealth in mutually exclusive terms: "No one can serve two masters. Either you will hate the one and love the other, or you will be loyal to the one and have contempt for the other. You cannot serve God and wealth" (Matthew 6:24). The Collyer brothers were a tragic demonstration of his warning:

> "Don't hoard treasure down here where it gets
> eaten by moths and corroded by rust or—worse!—
> stolen by burglars. Stockpile treasure in heaven,
> where it's safe from moth and rust and burglars.
> It's obvious, isn't it? The place where your treasure
> is, is the place you will most want to be, and end
> up being." (Matthew 6:19-21 *The Message*)

Paul gave the same warning to Timothy when he wrote that people who "set their hearts on being wealthy expose themselves to temptation. They fall into one of the world's traps...which are quite capable of utterly ruining and destroying their souls" (1 Timothy 6:9 JBP).

John Wesley underscored the same concern in his "discourses" on the Sermon on the Mount and in his later sermons, "The Danger of Riches," "The Rich Man and Lazarus," and "On the Danger of Increasing Riches," all of which built on themes he had described in his sermon, "The Use of Money."

If the Collyer brothers are a tragic picture of the foolishness of hoarding, Dorothy Ebersbach was a witness to the wisdom of saving.

THE WISDOM OF SAVING

Dorothy Ebersbach was the only person I've known who received the Congressional Gold Medal, the highest civilian honor that Congress can give. She was one of the most fascinating women I've known.

Dorothy was born in 1914. On a family trip to the 1933 Chicago World's Fair, she flew with her father in a seaplane. The thrill of that experience never left her. She earned her private pilot's license in 1939, three years after she graduated *summa cum laude* from Ohio University. Her father, a land developer in Tampa, Florida, gave her a Piper Cruiser, a single-engine plane that she used to deliver supplies around the state for the family business.

After Pearl Harbor, Dorothy became one of the 1,800 women who formed the Women's Airforce Service Pilots (WASP). Nearly half of the women who began WASP training didn't make it through basic training, but Dorothy did. She spent the war years ferrying new planes from factories to military bases, testing newly repaired planes, and towing targets for the male pilots to practice their dog-fight skills. In 2010, Dorothy and her fellow WASPs were awarded the Congressional Gold Medal for their service. Expressing her genuine humility, she said, "I was surprised. It was more than I expected to receive."

After the war, Dorothy graduated from the nursing school at Case Western Reserve University, returned to Tampa, and worked as a public health nurse until her retirement in 1975. It demonstrated both her love of nursing and her commitment to the welfare of the community.

Early in life, Dorothy's father taught her the wisdom of saving and investing. Though she never earned a large salary, she used her money wisely and invested carefully. She lived modestly in the house that her father built in the 1930s. Across the years, her wise investments grew. As a lifelong Methodist, she consistently supported the ministry of the church with her financial commitment.

Dorothy had a passionate commitment to higher education. When Lloyd Knox, her former pastor, was elected a bishop of The United Methodist Church, she was able to fund a scholarship in his honor at his alma mater. When she died in 2011, her estate completed a $4.7 million donation to Case Western to establish the Dorothy Ebersbach Academic Center for Flight Nursing, combining her passion for flying, nursing, and education.

Dorothy's bequest to Hyde Park United Methodist Church was the largest donation ever made to the church's endowment fund, establishing scholarships for young persons growing up in the church and for seminary students preparing for ministry. Another part of her estate provided ongoing support for the local food bank, the Florida United Methodist Children's Home, and the Florida United Methodist youth camp. Though she never married or had children of her own, generations of youth will be blessed by her visionary stewardship.

With all of that, the best things I will remember about Dorothy are her infectious laughter, the way her smile spread across her face, and the relentless joy that flowed through her life.

MAKING WISE INVESTMENTS

I picture Dorothy when I'm reading about the wise woman in Proverbs 31 who "surveys a field and acquires it; / from her own resources, she plants a vineyard" (31:16). A vineyard is a long-term investment. It takes years for a new vineyard to produce grapes. It doesn't turn a quick profit. It's the kind of patient investment that Jesus compared to a farmer who "scatters seed on the ground, then sleeps and wakes night and day. The seed sprouts and grows" (Mark 4:26-27).

Dorothy was like the wise investors in Jesus' story of the master who was going on a trip and entrusted his wealth to his servants: five coins (talents) to one servant, two coins to the second, and one coin to the third, "according to that servant's ability" (Matthew 25:14-30). The first and second servants both invested their coins and doubled their value. But the third servant "dug a hole in the ground and buried his master's money." He did absolutely nothing to increase the value of the master's gift.

When the master returned to settle accounts, the servants who had multiplied the value of the master's investment heard the master say, "You are a good and faithful servant! You've been faithful over a little. I'll put you in charge of much. Come, celebrate with me." When the third servant returned the coin just the way he had received it, the master called him an "evil and lazy servant." He went on, "You should have turned my money over to the bankers so that when I returned, you could give me what belonged to me with interest." (Every banker I know loves this parable!)

The master took the coin from the third servant and gave it to the first one saying, "Those who have much will receive more, and they will have more than they need. But as for those who don't have much, even the little bit they have will be taken away from them."

It's a stern parable that communicates the truth in Wesley's instruction when he said, "Having gained all you can, by honest wisdom, and unwearied diligence, the second rule of Christian prudence is, 'Save all you can.'"[1] We can feel the strength in Wesley's conviction when we read his words:

> Do not throw the precious talent into the sea....
> Do not throw it away in idle expenses, which is
> just the same as throwing it into the sea. Expend
> no part of it merely to gratify the desire of the
> flesh, the desire of the eye, or the pride of life.[2]

In his sermons on money, Wesley used two biblical words as the foundation for his teachings: *steward* and *prudence*. Let's explore those words and what they meant to Wesley.

The Faithful Steward

The Greek word we translate as "steward" is *oikonomos*. This was the title for the person who managed financial affairs for the head of the household or proprietor of the business. The steward was usually a freeborn man or a freed slave, which would indicate that the steward had some measure of personal discretion in the goods and money entrusted to him, although these items were still owned by the master.[3]

Jesus used this word when he asked the rhetorical question, "Who are the faithful and wise managers (*oikonomos*) whom the master will put in charge of his household servants, to give them their food at the proper time?" Jesus answered his own question by saying, "Happy are the servants whom the master finds fulfilling their responsibilities when he comes. I assure you that the master will put them in charge of all his possessions" (Luke 12:42-44).

In his sermon "The Use of Money," Wesley said "the ground and reason" for his teachings on money was our role as stewards.

> The Possessor of heaven and earth brought you
> into being, and placed you in this world…not as a
> proprietor, but a steward: As such he entrusted you,
> for a season, with goods of various kinds;
> but the sole property of these still rests in him….
> As you yourself are not your own, but his,
> such is, likewise, all that you enjoy. Such is
> your soul and your body, not your own, but
> God's. And so is your substance in particular.
> And he has told you, in the most clear and

express terms, how you are to employ it for
him, in such a manner, that it may be all an holy
sacrifice, acceptable through Christ Jesus.[4]

Wesley expanded this teaching about money in his
sermon "The Good Steward" when he pointed out the
difference between a "debtor" and a "steward."

We are now indebted to Him for all we have;
but although a debtor is obliged to return what
he has received, yet until the time of payment
comes, he is at liberty to use it as *he* pleases. It is
not so with a steward; he is not at liberty to use
what is lodged in his hands as he pleases, but as
his master pleases.... For he is not the proprietor
of any of these things, but barely entrusted with
them by another.... Now, this is exactly the case
of every man, with relation to God. We are not
at liberty to use what he has lodged in our hands
as we please, but as he pleases, who alone is the
possessor of heaven and earth, and the Lord of
every creature. We have no right to dispose of
anything we have, but according to His will, seeing
we are not proprietors of any of these things.[5]

Wesley said we are called to be faithful stewards of
our souls, our bodies, our speech, our hands and feet,
our talents, our time, and, specifically, our money.

> Above all, he has committed to our charge that
> precious talent which contains all the rest,—
> money: Indeed it is unspeakably precious, if
> we are wise and faithful stewards of it; if we
> employ every part of it for such purposes as
> our blessed Lord has commanded us to do.[6]

These teachings were not original to Mr. Wesley. Throughout church history, the beginning point for every understanding of Christian stewardship has been that everything we are and have is a gift from God. That is, the stuff I have—my money, my possessions, my talents, my body—are not my own. They belong to God, the giver of "every good and perfect gift" (James 1:17 KJV). They are given to me by the God who trusts me to use everything I am and have in ways that are consistent with the will and way of God. As a result, the transformative question for Christian stewards is always: Who really owns it?

That question is what the rich farmer was missing in Jesus' parable, described in the previous chapter (Luke 12:13-21). Don't miss the repetition of the word *my* when he says, "I have no place to store *my* harvest! . . . I'll tear down *my* barns and build bigger ones. That's where I'll store all *my* grain and goods" (Luke 12:17-18, italics added). In the NRSV translation, the rich farmer even says "*my* soul."

The farmer actually seems to believe he is solely responsible for his good fortune, as if he had raised the bumper crop by his own power with no contribution from the earth, the sun, and the rain; as if he had planted and harvested it single-handedly and owed nothing to the laborers in the fields; as if he had constructed bigger barns without builders and had hauled in the harvest on roads he had paved; as if he owed nothing to anyone else for his success. Jesus' makes the point that you'd have to be a fool to believe that!

At the center of a biblical perspective on money and possessions is a deep awareness that none of it really belongs to us. There is no such thing as "self-made" success. We are stewards of things that have been placed in our hands by an extravagantly generous God who trusts us to use things that ultimately belong to God in ways that satisfy God's good intentions, not just our own.

THE PRUDENT MANAGER

Wesley's second biblical word is *prudence*. The words *prudence* or *prudent* appear ten times in the Proverbs (CEB). *Prudent* shows up in Luke 12:42 when Jesus asks, "Who then is the faithful and *prudent* manager..." (NRSV, italics added). It was a common word in Wesley's time, appearing sixty-two times in

Pilgrim's Progress, where it is personified as one of the spiritual guides for Pilgrim's journey. In 1805, the Roman Catholic Church named prudence as one of the cardinal virtues along with justice, fortitude, and temperance.[7] In the years since, however, the use of the word has been in steady decline. We don't talk much about prudence anymore.[8]

The English word comes from a Latin root *prūdēns* meaning "farsighted." A prudent person is defined as "practical and careful in providing for the future, exercising good judgment or common sense."[9]

The Hebrew sages used the Hebrew root word in personifying Wisdom to say:

> I, Wisdom, dwell with prudence;
> I have found knowledge and
> discretion. (Proverbs 8:12)

It's the word Wesley used in declaring "save all you can" as the "the second rule of Christian prudence."[10] It's the wisdom to manage our finances with a far-sighted view. It means making wise decisions about the way we use our money now, so it will provide for us in the future.

Walter Brueggemann accurately describes our present day as "the Culture of Now."[11] While previous generations understood the value of delayed gratification and were more likely to believe in saving, we boomers and the generations that follow us have been conditioned to believe we can have everything we want and we can have it *now*. The near collapse of the American economy at the turn of the twenty-first century was in large part the result of irresponsible mortgage lending that enabled people to purchase homes they could not really afford. The oppressive weight of credit card debt is the tragic consequence of making purchasing decisions on the basis of immediate satisfaction rather than on the prudence that sees current expenditures in the light of long-term financial goals.

Oseola McCarty demonstrated that kind of prudence. She was born in Wayne County, Mississippi, in 1908. Her mother was the cook for a prominent white family in Hattiesburg. Oseola was a student at Eureka Elementary School when her mother taught her to save. She began ironing other people's clothes and started putting a little bit of her small earnings into a savings account in the First Mississippi National Bank. She had to quit school in the sixth grade to take care of an elderly aunt and never went back. Oseola McCarty never married or had children of her own. She never owned a car. She walked everywhere she went and rode with friends to the Friendship Baptist Church.

Outside her church and the families whose laundry she washed and ironed for seventy-four years, no one had ever heard of Oseola McCarty until word got out that she had given $150,000 to establish a scholarship at the University of Southern Mississippi, a school that would not have admitted her in the days of segregation. "I'm too old to get an education," she said, "but they can. . . . I can't do everything, but I can do something to help somebody. And what I can do I will do. I wish I could do more."[12] When asked how she accumulated that much money, she said, "It wasn't hard. I didn't buy things I didn't need. . . . The Lord helped me, and he'll help you, too."[13]

Oseola McCarty was practicing the wisdom of Proverbs 13:11:

Riches gotten quickly will dwindle,
   but those who acquire them
   gradually become wealthy.

That's the wisdom of prudence—the careful, far-sighted management of what we have to meet our own needs while it grows to provide for us and to bless others in the future. A more contemporary word might be *frugality*. Being frugal does not mean being cheap or stingy. It means using whatever we have wisely and well to accomplish its best purpose.

In the aftermath of the economic crash a few years ago, I discovered a contemporary version of Wesleyan prudence in a *Time* magazine cover article titled "The New Frugality." The writer said that in the face of economic hardship, we boomers are "channeling our grandparents, who were taught, like a mantra, to use it up, wear it out, make it do, do without." The writer sounded like one of Wesley's preachers when he wrote:

> As we pick through the economic rubble, we may find that our riches have buried our treasures. Money does not buy happiness; Scripture asserts this, research confirms it. Once you reach the median level of income, roughly $50,000 a year, wealth and contentment go their separate ways, and studies find that a millionaire is no more likely to be happy than someone earning one-twentieth as much....A consumer culture invites us to want more than we can ever have; a culture of thrift invites us to be grateful for whatever we can get.[14]

Author and sales consultant Lisa Earle McLeod called frugality "the new cool" when she wrote, "The recession is now official—my teenager no longer shops at Abercrombie & Fitch." She used the old word *prudent* when she went on to say:

By bankrupting our economy with their greed
and corruption, the money men of Wall Street
have accomplished what Main Street moms
have been trying to do for decades. They've
shown our kids that consumption does not
equate to happiness, and they're forcing the next
generation to become more prudent with their
money.... It's the new trend, pass it along."[15]

YOU NEED A PLAN

Let's face it. Saving is difficult, particularly in a
culture that conditions us to expect immediate gratification. But it can be done.

The key to Oseola McCarty's story is that she had
a plan. She didn't have much, but over time, the little
she had was multiplied to become a blessing to generations of students in the years ahead. The Bible says
that's the way God works. God takes the little we save
and multiplies it to be used to bless others and to fill
our lives with joy.

It may come as a surprise to some folks to discover
that most of what the Bible teaches about money is
not for the sake of supporting the church; it's for the
sake of saving our souls. Biblical writers knew that
we need clear spiritual guidance about the use of our
resources if we ever are going to find the abundant life

that Jesus promised. If the best way to a man's heart is through his stomach, God knows that the best way to all our hearts is through our checkbooks (Matthew 6:21). The purpose of the biblical emphasis on money is to draw us into a deeper relationship with God through which we can be used by God to bless others.

One practical approach to managing money is called the 10-10-80 Plan. It goes like this:

- 10 percent for God
- 10 percent for the future
- 80 percent to live on with gratitude and joy

It's as simple (and as difficult) as that. The first 10 percent of our income goes to God's work in this world through the church. It's called the tithe. The Bible says it already belongs to God, so the question is whether we will give what belongs to God back to God. For followers of Jesus, the tithe should be the bare minimum of our giving, the basement of Christian stewardship beneath which we never allow our generosity to fall. It's an act of spiritual discipline that helps us organize our lives and our resources around our commitment to Christ.

The second 10 percent of our income goes to the future. It's what Wesley was talking about in this second rule for money. It's what we save in order to meet both the expected and unexpected needs of the future. It's what enabled Oseola McCarty to make that amazing gift for the education of poor children in Mississippi.

That leaves 80 percent for us to live on with gratitude and joy, in ways that are consistent with the claims of Christ on our lives. Wesley was perfectly clear that what we do with this portion of our income is to be just as clearly determined by our commitment to Christ as the first 20 percent.

The challenge in following the 10-10-80 Plan or any savings plan is that our culture encourages us to live beyond our income. For many of us, what keeps us from saving all we can is not the high cost of living, but the cost of high living. Many of us simply cannot leap directly to 10-10-80 Plan because of the financial commitments we have made in the past. But it is a goal we can move toward as we reorient what we earn and what we save.

Saving prudently is difficult because it calls for a radical reorganization of our lives, and that's exactly the point. It's nothing less than a conversion experience as we reorient our whole existence around the value of God's kingdom. It's in the conversion process that the power of God's spirit is released into our lives.

JUST DO IT!

Saving as much as we can is not easy. It means breaking with a culture that is intent on having us spend more than we earn. It calls for disciplined action. In the spirit of Wesley's advice, here is my own homegrown version of how to "save all you can."

Face the facts.

Responsible use of money always involves a ruthless inventory of what we earn and what we spend. To be stewards of God's resources, we must begin by taking a careful look at how much money is coming in compared with how much is going out. It's often surprising to learn exactly where the money is going. In my experience, when people take a thorough inventory of their income and expenses, they are surprised by how much they have, how much they spend, and how they spend it.

Learn from the wisdom of others.

Jesus told the story of a foolish builder who didn't calculate the cost of construction and was unable to finish his project (Luke 14:28-30). I've known preachers and churches that found themselves in the same predicament because they did not draw on the wisdom of financially trained people. In our personal lives, moving in the direction of more prudent spending and saving often requires the wisdom of a professional financial planner to help us make wise choices about what we spend now and how we save for the future.

Oseola McCarty's mother taught her to put small amounts of what she earned in a savings account. Somewhere along the way, the local bankers noticed that her account was growing and took an interest in her. They advised her to move her money into CDs and conservative mutual funds. (They also convinced her to buy an air conditioner for her home.) The bank's trust officer used dimes to assist her in planning the distribution of her estate: one dime for her church (10 percent), one dime each for three relatives (30 percent), and the remaining six dimes (60 percent) for Southern Mississippi University to assist students, primarily African Americans, who could not afford to attend. If advisors had shared that wisdom with her earlier in life, her bequests would have been even larger.

Simplify your spending.

Wesley said the first step toward saving is to provide for the reasonable needs of your family. Begin with the essentials: housing, food, clothing, transportation, and medical bills. In this process, be absolutely ruthless in sorting out things that are essential from things you can live without. Know the true value of everything you purchase.

Henry David Thoreau memorably wrote, "Our life is frittered away by detail....Simplicity, simplicity, simplicity!"[16] Margot Starbuck moved toward simplifying her family's life when she became aware of "the possibility that the 'good life' I'd been sold as an American consumer—owning anything my heart desired—might not be as good as its converse." She decided to get rid of a thousand things in her home. It took some time to sort out what family members actually needed and used from the things they didn't. There were multiple trips to the Salvation Army. Unused skateboards, baseball mitts, footballs, and helmets went to younger children in the neighborhood. A stack of board games that had not been played for years was set on the front porch, free for the taking.

She reported that the process was transformational for the entire family. In the end, no one missed any of the things they had let go. Their experience with simplifying forced them to distinguish between needs and wants, allowed them to become more intentional about every item they owned or bought, and enabled them to begin saving for the future. Starbuck reported that, finally, the process had an impact on her life as a disciple of Jesus Christ.

As a person who follows Jesus, I am now liberated to respond to his voice because I'm less tied to what I own.... Releasing physical objects from my home has had the spiritual effect of putting me in proper relationship with the ones that remain.... "Enough"—which used to seem so elusive—has come into clearer focus, I've seen the Provider more clearly and have felt freer to meet the needs of others.[17]

Do plastic surgery.

Develop a plan to get rid of credit card debt. If you are unable to pay off the credit card balance every month, cut up the cards and practice the discipline of not buying anything unless you can pay for it with cash.

Break the shopaholic addiction.

Avoid going shopping as a means of entertainment. Only go shopping when you have made a decision about what you intend to purchase. Buy it and get out of the mall before you are tempted to purchase a shopping basket full of unnecessary stuff.

Invest in your future.

Instead of seeing savings as money that is taken from you, train yourself to see it as money that is growing for you. Celebrate any increase in interest, even if those are pretty small these days.

You Can't Take It With You

A pastor friend told me about a woman who came to see him when the church he served was facing a major financial challenge. When she surprised him with a large check, he smiled and said, "Well, I guess you can't take it with you." She replied, "Believe me, I would if I could!"

I remember the first time I heard John Ortberg tell a story that later became the title of one of his best-selling books. It's the story of the day he beat his grandmother in Monopoly. He said it happened at Marvin Gardens, where he wiped her off the board. His grandmother had taught him to play the game, and now he had outplayed her. As he relished his victory, she taught him a far more important lesson with these words: When the game is over, it all goes back in the box.[18]

All the money, properties, houses, and hotels he had acquired weren't really his. They had been in the box before he played, and they would be there after he stopped. At the end of the day, it all goes back in the box.

However we express it, the truth is that we can't take it with us. Shrouds don't have pockets, and hearses don't pull U-Haul trailers. In Jesus' story of the foolish farmer, God said, "Fool, tonight you will die. Now who will get the things you have prepared for yourself?" (Luke 12:20).

It's a good question for every faithful steward to ask: Who will get these things? Who will acquire all that I have accumulated during my life? How will the things I leave behind bear witness to the faith I have tried to live? What does it mean for me to take Jesus seriously when he said, "Stop collecting treasures for your own benefit on earth, where moth and rust eat them and where thieves break in and steal them. Instead, collect treasures for yourselves in heaven, where moth and rust don't eat them and where thieves don't break in and steal them" (Matthew 6:19-29)? How can I invest now in things that will outlive me, things on earth that are consistent with the way things will be in heaven? What will those things be, and whose will they be?

Warren Buffet is one of the wealthiest men in America, but he doesn't intend to pass all his wealth on to his children. He wisely said, "My kids are going to carve out their own place in this world, and they know I'm for them whatever they want to do. Buffet goes on to say that setting his kids up with "a lifetime supply of food stamps just because they came out of the right womb" can be harmful for them and perhaps even be "an antisocial act." He intends to leave his children "enough money so that they would feel they could do anything, but not so much that they could do nothing."[19]

Mr. Buffet would have agreed with Mr. Wesley on this one. Wesley, in a time when wealth was passed on by inheritance in the aristocracy, gave this advice about inheritance:

> Why should you throw away money upon your
> children, any more than upon yourself, in delicate
> food, in gay or costly apparel, in superfluities of
> any kind? . . . Do not leave it to them to throw
> away. If you have good reason to believe that
> they would waste what is now in your possession
> in gratifying and thereby increasing the desire
> of the flesh, the desire of the eye, or the pride of
> life at the peril of theirs and your own soul, do
> not set these traps in their way. . . . How amazing
> then is the infatuation of those parents who think
> they can never leave their children enough![20]

Wesley asked himself an important question: "What would you do if you had a considerable fortune to leave?"

> If I had one child, elder or younger, who knew the
> value of money; one who I believed, would put
> it to the true use, I should think it my absolute,

97

indispensable duty to leave that child the bulk
of my fortune; and to the rest just so much as
would enable them to live in the manner they
had been accustomed to do. "But what [he asked
again] if all your children were equally ignorant
of the true use of money?" I ought then . . . to
give each what would keep him above want,
and to bestow all the rest in such a manner as I
judged would be most for the glory of God.[21]

I have a friend who probably doesn't realize how
closely he has followed Mr. Wesley's teaching. My
friend has three children who will be heirs to all he
has earned and saved. He has told his children, however, that there is a fourth heir who will receive an
equal percentage of his estate. The "fourth heir"
includes his church, along with mission and community agencies he has supported throughout his life as
the ongoing witness of his faith and values.

I've also known people who practiced the discipline of tithing throughout their lives and have written
into their will or estate plan that a tithe of everything
they leave behind will go to God's work in this world
after their deaths, just the way it was shared during
their lives.

We can't take it with us, but the things we save can
be used in ways that carry on the faith and values by
which we have lived.

BEGIN WITH THE END

Stephen Covey became a best-selling author with his book *The 7 Habits of Highly Effective People.* The second habit he named was "Begin with the End in Mind." Covey challenged his readers to use their imagination, which he defined as "the ability to envision in your mind what you cannot at present see with your eyes." He said what we become or accomplish will follow what we imagine, "just as a building follows a blueprint." He warned that if we don't make a conscious effort to visualize what we want for the future, we will be allowing other people or circumstances to determine it for us.

> Begin with the End in Mind means to begin
> each day, task, or project with a clear vision
> of your desired direction and destination,
> and then continue by flexing your proactive
> muscles to make things happen.[22]

Wesley's rule to "save all you can" is not a justification to accumulate wealth for its own sake or, like the foolish farmer who kept building himself larger barns, to satisfy a narrow addiction to comfort and self-satisfaction. Christian disciples save all they can as a spiritual practice enabling them to grow toward a greater end—namely, discovering how our resources can be used to bring about God's kingdom on earth as it is in heaven.

Saving is a practical step along the way toward Wesley's understanding of "Christian perfection," defined as loving God with all our heart, soul, mind, and strength and loving others the way we have been loved by God. Saving is a means by which every area of our life comes under the gracious rule of God's love in Jesus Christ.

Now, that is an end worth pursuing!

—4—

Give All You Can

Generous persons will prosper;
those who refresh others will
themselves be refreshed.
(Proverbs 11:25)

In his simple rules for the use of money, John Wesley's first rule was to "gain [earn] all you can." His second rule was to "save all you can." And his third rule, which we will discuss in this chapter, was to "give all you can."

To start the discussion, I'll call three witnesses: Big Daddy, from the Tennessee Williams play *Cat on a Hot Tin Roof*, and, from the Bible, Zacchaeus the tax collector, and a widow whose name we never learn.

Wisdom From Big Daddy

Big Daddy was a very rich man. The iconic Southern plantation owner had recently received a diagnosis of cancer that would end his life, and he told his son:

"I'm a rich man, Brick, yep, I'm a mighty rich
man. . . . Close to ten million in cash an' blue chip
stocks, outside, mind you, of twenty-eight thousand
acres of the richest land this side of the valley
Nile! But a man can't buy his life with it . . . he
can't buy back his life when his life is finished."[1]

Big Daddy, sounding a little bit like one of the biblical prophets, went on to say:

"The human animal is a beast that dies and if
he's got money he buys and buys and buys and
I think the reason he buys everything he can
buy is that in the back of his mind he has the
crazy hope that one of his purchases will be life
everlasting!—Which it never can be . . ."[2]

Big Daddy got it right. He had learned the wisdom
passed down to us by the Hebrew sages: "Those who
trust in their wealth will wither, / but the righteous
will thrive like leafy trees" (Proverbs 11:28). Jesus
reiterated that wisdom with a rhetorical question:
"Why would people gain the whole world but lose
their lives? What will people give in exchange for
their lives?" (Matthew 16:26).

Wesley expressed the same wisdom in his sermon
"The Danger of Riches."

102

> Suppose ye that money, though multiplied as the
> sand of the sea, can give happiness? Then you
> are "given up to a strong delusion to believe a
> lie;"—a palpable lie, confuted daily by a thousand
> experiments.... In seeking happiness from riches,
> you are only striving to drink out of empty cups.[3]

In our heart of hearts, we know that these warnings are true, even when we are tempted to "drink out of empty cups" in the illusion that simply increasing our wealth can satisfy the deepest longings of our souls. The warnings prepare us to hear Wesley's final instruction.

> Let not any man imagine that he has done anything,
> barely by going thus far, by "gaining and saving
> all he can," if he were to stop here. All this is
> nothing, if a man go not forward, if he does not
> point all this at a farther end. Nor, indeed, can a
> man properly be said to save anything, if he only
> lays it up. You may as well throw your money into
> the sea.... Not to use, is effectually to throw it
> away.... Add the Third rule to the two preceding.
> Having, First, gained all you can, and, Secondly
> saved all you can, Then "give all you can."[4]

This brings us to our second witness. It's a story that every child in Sunday school can tell or sing.

A Big Change for a Little Man

Zacchaeus (described in Luke 19:1-10) was a little man with a big bank account. Like Big Daddy, he was very rich. As chief tax collector, he profited from a corrupt economic system in which he collected more taxes to feed the voracious economic appetite of the Roman Empire from which he could extract a generous percentage for himself. As a result, he was despised as a rapacious sinner, rejected by his own people, and unwelcome in the synagogue.

Have you ever wondered why Zacchaeus climbed up into that sycamore tree to get a look at Jesus? How had he even heard of Jesus? Luke may have given us a clue earlier in his Gospel, when, in the fifth chapter, another tax collector named Levi, a.k.a. Matthew, threw a dinner party to introduce Jesus to "a large number of tax collectors" (Luke 5:29). I like to imagine that Zacchaeus was in that disreputable crowd.

If Zacchaeus was indeed at the dinner table with Jesus, he may have experienced something he never had known before. He would have felt accepted by Jesus and loved by God. He could have glimpsed a life that was about more than grabbing all the money he could get. He may have realized that all his wealth could never buy the life he most deeply desired.

Perhaps he became convinced there was a higher calling for the way he used his money.

When Zacchaeus heard that Jesus was coming through Jericho on his way to Jerusalem, he may also have heard the prediction that when Jesus entered the city he would be rejected and put to death (Luke 18:31-33). If that were true, then this might be Zacchaeus' only chance to see Jesus again.

So there he was, willing to sacrifice his pride and dignity by hanging on for dear life in the branches of that sycamore tree. He must have looked downright foolish! I suspect he nearly fell off the limb when Jesus called him by name: "Zacchaeus, get down here! I'm going to your house today!" (Luke 19:5, author's paraphrase).

It's probably an understatement when Luke says that Zacchaeus was "happy to welcome Jesus." But it would be no understatement for Luke to record that everyone else "grumbled" at the idea of Jesus hanging out with an obvious sinner like Zacchaeus (19:6-7).

In response to the unexpected, undeserved, unearned grace of God in Jesus Christ, Zacchaeus blurted out, "Wow! The only way I know to say 'Thanks' is to give half my wealth to the poor and pay back the folks I've cheated four times over!" Jesus said, "Now, that's what salvation looks like! Let's party!" (Luke 19:8-10, author's paraphrase).

Like Big Daddy, little Zacchaeus discovered that there is more to life than earning and saving. Unlike Big Daddy, though, Zacchaeus experienced salvation.

Zacchaeus' witness underscores the deep reality that salvation is not merely a spiritual experience that prepares us for life after death. Salvation is the way God transforms every area of life so that we become a part of God's saving work in this world. Salvation changes our hearts by changing the fundamental orientation of our living, including the way we use our money. It sets us free from bondage to narrow self-interest and opens our lives to the way the Spirit of God can be at work through us in the lives of others.

Salvation is, of course, about a lot more than money, but it is never about anything less than money, particularly in a culture that is compulsively driven by the power of money, a culture in which money has such awesome power as a blessing or curse, as a gracious gift we manage for God's sake, or as a demonic tyrant that manages us for its own sake.

Martin Luther, the sixteenth-century reformer, said that three conversions are necessary in the Christian life: conversion of the heart, of the mind, and of the purse.[5] The fact that Luther put the purse last on the list may suggest that he realized just how slow we are to allow that particular type of conversion to happen, or, like Wesley, he may have seen the movement toward generosity as a later development in our journey to salvation, just as it was for Zacchaeus.

Zacchaeus did not earn salvation by giving. His newfound generosity was his response to the extravagant generosity of God. But salvation never would have become a reality for Zacchaeus without his movement from a life that was consumed with gaining and saving into a life that was energized by giving.

THE WIDOW'S MITE

Our third witness has almost nothing in common with either Big Daddy or Zacchaeus. She is a woman, she is a widow, she is poor, and she is nameless. Both Mark and Luke tell her story (Mark 12:41-44; Luke 21:1-4), but neither mentions her name.

It seems that Jesus was doing some serious people-watching in the Temple. Mark says that Jesus, as he watched, observed the way people gave their offerings. (On a side note, this raises the disturbing question of how much we would put in the offering plate if we knew Jesus was watching us...which, of course, he is!) Thirteen large, metal, trumpet-shaped containers lined the wall of the Temple courtyard. Because there was no paper money, we can imagine that when the rich dropped a large gift into the container, you could hear it clanging all the way to the bottom.

Jesus watched—and heard—the way the rich gave their gifts, "throwing in lots of money" (Mark 12:41). Then he noticed an anonymous widow who dropped two tiny coins into the offering. The original text says the coins were *lepta*, the smallest Greek coins of the day, which were so small that you couldn't hear a sound when they hit the bottom of the container. The translators of the King James Version figured the equivalent in seventeenth-century English currency and wrote that she gave "two mites" (Luke 21:2 KJV), thereby carving into church history the story of "the widow's mite."

Jesus told his disciples, "I assure you that this poor widow has put in more than everyone who's been putting money in the treasury. All of them are giving out of their spare change. But she from her hopeless poverty has given everything she had, even what she needed to live on" (Mark 12:43-44).

Clearly, Jesus had a different way of counting the offering that day. He counted it

- based not on its size but on its impact on the giver;
- based not on the difference it made in the Temple treasury but on the difference it made in the giver's life;
- based not on how much people gave but on how much they had left over afterward;

- based not on other offerings but on the capacity of the giver.

Jesus said that some of the people that day "contributed out of their abundance" (12:44 NRSV). In other words, they never felt it. It never made a dent in the way they lived or used their resources. But this woman gave out of her poverty. It had a direct impact on the way she lived the rest of her life; indeed, it represented a total reordering of her existence around her faith in God.

When pastor and author William Sloane Coffin preached on the story of the generous widow, he said she "gave more than she could spare. She gave until she felt the pinch. She gave until she felt the hurt. No, she gave until it felt good! How much should we give? The only safe rule is to give more than we can spare. For only then do we finally give ourselves."[6]

Note that the point of Jesus' story was not to disparage, discourage, or diminish the generosity of people who are willing and able to give large gifts. Jesus was not saying that small gifts are more important than large ones or that small gifts are evidence of someone inherently more spiritual or righteous than larger ones. The reality is that large gifts are necessary in order to sustain the ongoing ministry of the church so that smaller gifts can be maximized in their use.

Far from criticizing large givers, Wesley encouraged and to some degree depended on them. Selina Shirley Hastings, Countess of Huntingdon (1707-1791), was called "Lady Bountiful" for her generous support of the Methodist movement. Her gifts built sixty-four Methodist chapels, supported early missionary work in America, and established the first Methodist theological college.[7]

I give thanks for faithful disciples such as Lady Huntingdon, who out of their abundance are able to provide abundantly for the work of the kingdom of God in the congregations and communities I've served. I've seen their large gifts undergird the organizational structures that provide food, clothing, and shelter for homeless people. I know pastors who are in ministry today because generous givers provided scholarships for their seminary education. I've seen the way generous endowments enable vital ministry to continue through seismic shifts in the economy.

The problem for large givers, however, is not the size of the gift but the size of the ego when giving in ways that draw attention to themselves. By contrast, I praise God for the humble generosity of faithful disciples who are able to drop gifts—of any size—into the offering plate as a part of their spiritual discipline. This kind of giving must have been what Jesus had in mind when he said,

"Whenever you give to the poor, don't blow your
trumpet as the hypocrites do in the synagogues
and in the streets so that they may get praise
from people.... But when you give to the poor,
don't let your left hand know what your right
hand is doing so that you may give to the poor
in secret. Your Father who sees what you do
in secret will reward you." (Matthew 6:2-4)

With us as with the widow, Jesus counts our offerings based not on the size of the gift but on the impact it has on the giver. He looks at our giving based not on how much we give but on how much is left over after we give it.

GIVING FOR THE JOY OF IT

New York Times columnist Nicholas Kristof and his wife Sheryl WuDunn studied current patterns of giving and came to the same conclusion as John Wesley. Writing from a secular perspective in their book *A Path Appears*, they confirm what the Bible said all along—namely, that giving is good for us and can be a source of joy. They use neuroscience to demonstrate that we experience a "happiness boost" from our efforts to help others. Their conclusion is that "doing good is a good deal."[8]

Big Daddy, little Zacchaeus, and the poor widow all bear witness in their own way to the joy that comes when we learn how to give all we can. So does a fourth witness: Ebenezer Scrooge, the wonderful character from *A Christmas Carol* whose self-absorbed greed is transformed into joyful generosity.

It's unfortunate that Charles Dickens's classic story gets tucked away with the decorations, seldom to be seen until we set up the Christmas tree again. Writing out of his painful observations about the ravages of poverty in his own time, Dickens captured the joy of Scrooge's salvation that surely was the eventual result of his generosity.

> [Scrooge] became as good a friend, as good a master, and as good a man, as the good old city knew, or any other good old city, town, or borough, in the good old world. Some people laughed to see the alteration in him, but he let them laugh, and little heeded them; for he was wise enough to know that nothing ever happened on this globe, for good, at which some people did not have their fill of laughter in the outset; and knowing that such as these would be blind anyway, he thought it quite as well that they should wrinkle up their eyes in grins, as have the malady in less attractive forms. His own heart laughed: and that was quite enough for him.[9]

A FARTHER END

We concluded last week with Stephen Covey's encouragement to "Begin with the End in Mind." In the same way, John Wesley was clear that earning and saving are not ends in themselves. They lead toward what Wesley called the "farther end" of giving.

Wesley acknowledged that when it comes to making the best use of money, "the children of this world are in their generation wiser than the children of light" (Luke 16:8 KJV), and faithful people often do not "employ it to the greatest advantage." In all his sermons on money, Wesley affirmed the importance of providing for personal and family needs. Because of his passionate engagement with the poor, he knew there was no inherent goodness in poverty. Life is better when we have what Wesley called "things needful for yourself . . . for your wife, your children, your servants, or any others who pertain to your household."[10]

Wesley was equally clear that simply earning and saving can, in fact, become an impediment to "going on to perfection" as a follower of Christ unless these practices become the means by which we move toward "a farther end," which is a life of Christ-centered generosity in which we find joy in giving all we can.

The urgency behind Wesley's sermon "The Use of Money" was his pastoral desire to lead people into a healthier, more productive, more deeply Christ-centered life by providing practical wisdom on the relationship between their faith and their finances. Wesley's rules are not about raising money for the church; they are about becoming more like Jesus. His intention was to guide the early Methodists in the spiritual discipline of generosity so they would become a giving people whose lives were shaped in the likeness of an extravagantly generous God.

The "farther end" toward which Wesley sought to move us is a life that fulfills God's best purpose for the use of our resources and equips us to participate in God's loving, saving, healing work in this world. It is a practical expression of Wesley's teaching on "Christian perfection" as the ongoing process by which the Holy Spirit continues God's work of salvation in and through us. (For a deeper understanding of Wesley's teachings on Christian perfection, see my Abingdon study *A Disciple's Heart*.[11])

The words in Wesley's sermon convey the same urgency as Paul's words to his protégé, Timothy:

> Tell those rich in this world's wealth to quit
> being so full of themselves and so obsessed
> with money.... Tell them to go after God, who
> piles on all the riches we could ever manage—
> to do good, to be rich in helping others, to be
> extravagantly generous. If they do that, they'll

build a treasury that will last, gaining life that is truly life. (1 Timothy 6:17–19, *The Message*)

Paul's call to extravagant generosity and Wesley's call to give all we can are about more than just writing an occasional check to our church or our favorite charity. They define a reordering of financial priorities around our commitment to Christ. This reordering includes a biblical vision of economic justice in which everyone shares in the abundant life God intends for all people. It's a call to economic practices by which we experience "life that is truly life."

The "farther end" is to see the ways our money may be

of unspeakable service . . . and (if we use it according to Christian wisdom) of doing all manner of good . . . answering the noblest ends . . . food for the hungry, drink for the thirsty, raiment for the naked . . . a defence for the oppressed, a means of health to the sick, of ease to them that are in pain; it may be as eyes to the blind, as feet to the lame; yea, a lifter up from the gates of death![12]

In fact, the "farther end" to which Wesley calls us is nothing less than using our money as the practical means by which we participate in God's kingdom coming on earth, even as it is already fulfilled in heaven. It's a way of embracing the love of God that walked among us in Jesus Christ and helping to ensure that that love remains a down-to-earth, human reality in this world.

CHARITY OR STEWARDSHIP?

Pastoral experience has taught me the difference between charitable giving and Christian stewardship. Charity is a compassionate, generous, and appropriate response to a specific need. For followers of Christ, it is a practical expression of Jesus' love and it is a beautiful thing to see. Stewardship is a different deal. It represents a radical reorientation of our whole life—including our finances—around a commitment to Christ. Here are some comparisons to ponder:

- Charity can happen in a moment; stewardship takes a lifetime.
- Charity may cause us to give out of our abundance; stewardship changes the financial priorities by which we live.
- Effective charity is measured by the difference it makes for the ones who receive it; stewardship is measured by the difference it makes in the life of the giver.

116

- Charity is a compassionate response to an immediate need; stewardship is a spiritual discipline that enables us to grow toward "the farther end" of a life that is "fully grown, measured by the standard of the fullness of Christ" (Ephesians 4:13).

In a sermon at the Riverside Church in New York City, William Sloane Coffin acknowledged that if he were a person in the pew who heard the new preacher announce his subject as stewardship, he might have joined the critics who "wonder testily why churches always have to spoil everything by harping constantly on the need for more money."[13] But Coffin, like Wesley, went on to define stewardship "as an end—a goal—of all life itself."[14]

As part of his sermon, Coffin read 1 Peter 4:10 (NRSV): "Like good stewards of the manifold grace of God, serve one another with whatever gift each of you has received." Closing his Bible, Coffin preached, "That's what we're here on earth to do: to dispense God's grace in its varied forms.... Stewardship, in short, consists in living a Christ-life life; it is not a part-time affair of a few church-related folk, but a full-time calling for the whole human species."[15]

The Ways We Give

So, how do we give all we can? What are the practices by which we grow toward the "farther end" of a joyfully generous life?

In our journey to joyful giving, we begin as *tossers*. That's the word Eugene Peterson uses to describe the people, observed by Jesus in the Temple, who "tossed money in for the collection" (Mark 12:41, *The Message*). We toss our gifts, whatever their size, into the offering plate in worship or into the red kettles around Christmas the way folks did that day in the Temple.

It's what I do when I'm a visitor in a congregation other than the one in which I live out my discipleship. I'll confess that my generosity has been stretched when I open my wallet to discover that the smallest bill in my possession is $20. "Tossing" is giving off the edge. We never miss what we give in this way. It never makes a difference in our lives, though by the miracle of God's grace it can be used to make a difference in the lives of others.

As we grow in the spiritual discipline of giving, we become *tryers*. For many faithful disciples, a cold-turkey leap to tithing is impossible because of their current financial condition or the amount of debt they have incurred across the years. They know that moving toward the biblical discipline of tithing is a huge step, calling for major readjustment of their budget. *Tryers* are folks who lay out a plan for a systematic process to move from where they are to where they believe God would like them to be. They grow one step at a time toward the goal of tithing by reducing debt and reorganizing their financial priorities as they grow.

Finally, reaching the "farther end" toward which financial discipleship leads, we become *tithers*. Tithing is the base line or beginning point of a generous life. A lay leader in my last congregation often reminded us that in developing a generous life, tithing is a great place to begin but a terrible place to stop.

Giving the first 10 percent of our resources back to the God who gave them to us enables us to live into the command, "Honor the LORD with your wealth / and with the first of all your crops" (Proverbs 3:9). Tithing is a practice rooted in God's instructions in Deuteronomy:

> When you have come into the land that the LORD your God is giving you as an inheritance to possess, . . . you shall take some of the first of all the fruit of the ground, which you harvest from the land that the LORD your God is giving you, and you shall put it in a basket and go to the place that the LORD your God will choose as a dwelling for his name. (Deuteronomy 26:1-2, NRSV)

The ancient Hebrews gave, not as a duty or obligation, but out of sheer gratitude for all they had received from God. They gave in a joyful festival with great food, strong drink, and dancing. It became a tangible way of ordering their lives around their relationship with God.

An attorney friend suddenly lost his job and with it the entire family income. He and his wife were prayerfully searching for wisdom to find their way through their financial crisis. He had heard about tithing but had never taken that step as a spiritual discipline. He said, "I realized that 10 percent of nothing is nothing, so there was never a better time to begin." He and his family rebuilt their financial life around their commitment to Christ and have continued to grow in their faith, generosity, and joy.

Where are you on the journey to the farther end of Christ-shaped generosity? Are you a tosser, a tryer, or a tither? There are challenges at each stage of the journey.

- To the *tossers*, the challenge is to take the first step toward a disciplined approach to giving, in light of our commitment to Christ.
- To the *tryers*, the challenge is to keep moving into a deeper level of stewardship, as we

      reorient our priorities around the values and vision of God's kingdom.

- To the *tithers*, the challenge is to keep moving beyond tithing and into a life of abundant generosity.

The promise of the Proverbs is clear:

Those who give generously receive more,
    but those who are stingy with what
    is appropriate will grow needy.
Generous persons will prosper;
    those who refresh others will themselves
    be refreshed. (Proverbs 11:24-25)

IF YOU COULD ASK GOD FOR ANYTHING

We began this study with Stanley Johnson, who did not need more money so much as he needed more wisdom in how to use it. I wonder if Stanley ever caught on.

Stanley's quandary brings us back to Solomon's dream, described in the introduction to this book, in which God said, "Ask whatever you wish, and I'll give it to you" (1 Kings 3:5). Solomon could have asked for royal power, ever-increasing wealth, or the defeat of his enemies. He could have asked for protection for his wives and concubines. But, as we learned, Solomon knew what he needed most. He asked for wisdom. As a result, God gave Solomon all he requested and more: wealth, fame, and a long life.

I wonder if Solomon's spirit was in the background when Jesus said, "Desire first and foremost God's kingdom and God's righteousness, and all these things will be given to you as well" (Matthew 6:33). It may have been what C. S. Lewis had in mind when he wrote, "Aim at Heaven and you will get Earth 'thrown in'; aim at Earth and you will get neither."[16] As the Hebrew sages might have put it, when we find wisdom, we find everything we need to live a healthy, whole, productive life.

We can read Solomon's story as one event that happened on one particular night in one particular place. But my sense is that, for Christians, the request for wisdom is not a one-time event, especially related to the use of our money. It becomes a life pattern in which we constantly are searching for divine wisdom.

If you could ask God for anything, what would it be? May it be the gift of wisdom to use what John Wesley called the "excellent gift" of money in ways that fulfill God's highest and best purpose for us and for the world in which we live.

NOTES

Introduction

1. Walter Brueggemann, *Sabbath as Resistance: Saying No to the Culture of Now* (Louisville: Westminster John Knox Press, 2014), xii, 13.

2. T. S. Eliot, *Choruses from 'The Rock', I,* in *The Complete Poems and Plays of T.S. Eliot* (London: Faber & Faber, 1969), 147.

3. George Gershwin and Ira Gershwin, *I Got Rhythm,* http://artists.letssingit.com/george-gershwin-lyrics-i-got-rhythm-qq9g1s5#axzz3NNG1f2Ll.

4. Harry Emerson Fosdick, "God of Grace and God of Glory," *The United Methodist Hymnal* (Nashville: The United Methodist Publishing House, 1986) 577, stanza 3.

5. Peter Storey, *And Are We Yet Alive? Revisioning Our Wesleyan Heritage in a New Southern Africa* (Cape Town: Methodist Publishing House, 2004), 44-45.

6. John Wesley, "The Use of Money," Sermon 50, http://www.umcmission.org/Find-Resources/John-Wesley-Sermons/Sermon-50-The-Use-of-Money, Intro., 2.

7. Ibid., III, 1.

8. Ibid.

9. Charles Wesley, "Come, Wisdom, Power, and Grace Divine," *Hymns for the Use of the Methodist Episcopal Church: Revised Edition* (New York: Carlton & Lanham/ Cincinnati: Hitchcock & Walden, 1869) 717, stanzas 1 and 5.

Chapter 1: We Don't Need More Money; We Need Wisdom

1. Lending Tree. "Stanley Johnson." Television advertisement. Mullen. 1999. http://www.youtube.com/watch?v=r0HX4a5P8eE.

2. *The Anchor Bible Dictionary*, David Noel Freedman, editor (New York: Doubleday, 1992), Vol. 6, 920.

3. Ellen Davis, *Getting Involved with God: Rediscovering the Old Testament* (Boston: Cowley Publications, 2001), 95.

4. Ibid., 91.

5. Ibid., 92.

6. deClaissé-Walford, Nancy L. "Proverbs." In *The CEB Study Bible with Apocrypha*, ed. Joel B. Green. (Nashville: Common English Bible, 2011), 1005.

7. *Anchor Bible Dictionary*, 925.

8. *Getting Involved with God*, 89.

9. "Yaré" http://www.biblestudytools.com/lexicons/hebrew/nas/yare .html.

10. Ibid.

11. *Getting Involved with God*, 103.

12. "Wise," http://bible.oremus.org/?ql=290151447; "wisdom," http://bible.oremus.org/?ql=290151643; "fool," http://bible. oremus.org/?ql=290151892; and "foolish," http://bible.oremus. org/?ql=290151953.

13. Eric Hobsbawm, "Methodism and the Threat of Revolution in Britain," *History Today*, Volume 7, Issue 5, May 1957, http://www .historytoday.com/eric-hobsbawm/methodism-and-threat -revolution-britain.

14. "The Use of Money," Intro., 2.

15. Ibid.

16. Ibid.

Chapter 2: Earn All You Can

1. John Bunyan, *Pilgrim's Progress*, 1678, Chapter 23. Printed for Nath. Ponder at the Peacock in the Poulerey, near Cornhil,

2. "The Use of Money," Intro., 2.

3. Ibid.

4. Ibid.

5. Ibid., I, 1, 7.

6. Jem Lugo, "Rejected and approved speeches of Springstead valedictorian Jem Lugo," *Tampa Bay Times*, June 4, 2009, http://www .tampabay.com/news/education/k12/rejected-and-approved-speeches -of-springstead-valedictorian-jem-lugo/1007369

7. "The Use of Money," I, 7.

8. Martin Luther, *The Babylonian Captivity of the Church*, quoted by Greg Ayers, in "Martin Luther's View of Faith & Work," Institute for Faith, Work & Economics, http://blog.tifwe.org/martin-luthers-view -of-faith-work/.

9. John Ellerton, "Behold Us, Lord, a Little Space," *The Methodist Hymnal* (Nashville: The United Methodist Publishing House, 1964), 549, stanzas 3-6.

10. James C. Collins and Jerry I. Porras, *Built to Last: Successful Habits of Visionary Companies* (New York: Harper Business, 1994), 8.

11. "The Use of Money," I, 7.

12. Richard P. Heitzenrater. *Wesley and the People Called Methodists* (Nashville: Abingdon, Second Edition, 2013), 242-243.

13. "The Use of Money," I, 8.

14. Ibid.

15. Jim Collins, *Good to Great: Why Some Companies Make the Leap . . . and Others Don't* (New York: Harper Business, 2001), 1.

16. Ibid., 128.

17. Ibid., 13, 21.

18. "The Use of Money," I, 1

19. Ibid.

20. Ibid.

21. "Sabbath," http://www.biblestudytools.com/dictionaries/smiths -bible-dictionary/sabbath.html.

22. *Sabbath as Resistance: Saying No to the Culture of Now*, xiii-xiv.

23. "The Use of Money," I, 2.

24. Ibid.

25. Ibid.

26. William Sloane Coffin, *The Collected Sermons of William Sloane Coffin: The Riverside Years, Vol. 2* (Louisville: John Knox Press, 2008), 75.

27. Robert Schlesinger, "The Origins of That Eisenhower 'Every Gun That Is Made . . .' Quote," *US News & World Report*, Sept. 30, 2011, http://www.usnews.com/opinion/blogs/robert -schlesinger/2011/09/30/the-origins-of-that-eisenhower -every-gun-that-is-made-quote.

28. John Wesley, "The Good Steward," Sermon 51, http://www .umcmission.org/Find-Resources/John-Wesley-Sermons /Sermon-51-The-Good-Steward, I, 1.

29. John Wesley, "The More Excellent Way," Sermon 89, http://www
.umcmission.org/Find-Resources/John-Wesley-Sermons/Sermon
-89-The-More-Excellent-Way; III, 1.

30. Ibid.

31. Ibid., III, 2.

32. Ibid., III, 3.

33. Charles Wesley, "Summoned My Labour to Renew," *Hymns
for Divine Worship Compiled for the Use of The Methodist New
Connexion* (London: William Cooke, Methodist New Connexion
Book-Room, 1863) 685, stanzas 1-3.

Chapter 3: Save All You Can

1, "The Use of Money," II, 1.

2. Ibid.

3. "Oikonomos," http://biblehub.com/greek/3623.htm.

4. "The Use of Money," III, 2.

5. "The Good Steward," I, 1.

6. Ibid., I, 7.

7. *Catechism of the Catholic Church*, Article 7, The Virtues, http://www
.vatican.va/archive/ccc_css/archive/catechism/p3s1c1a7.htm.

8. Decline in use of prudence, https://books.google.com/ngrams/
graph?content=prudence&year_start=1800&year
_end=2000&corpus=15&smoothing=3&share=&direct
_url=t1%3B%2Cprudence%3B%2Cc0.

9. "Prudent," The Free Dictionary, http://www.thefreedictionary.com/
prudent.

10. "The Use of Money," II, 1.

11. *Sabbath as Resistance: Saying No to the Culture of Now,* iii.

12. Sharon Wertz, "Oseola McCarty Donates $150,000 to Southern
Miss," *The University of Southern Mississippi Office of University
Communications* (The University Southern Mississippi, June 26,
1995; accessed February 2, 2015) available from http://www.usm
.edu/news/archives/older/oola1.htm.

13. Selena Maranjian, "The Oseola McCarty Fribble," *The Motley Fool*
(The Motley Fool, LLC, September 28, 1999; accessed February 2,
2015); available from www.fool.com/fribble/1999/fribble990928
.htm.

14. Nancy Gibbs, "The Great Recession: America Becomes Thrift Nation," *Time*, April 15, 2009, http://content.time.com/time/nation /article/0,8599,1891527,00.html

15. Lisa Earle McLeod, "Teen Trends: Is Fiscal Prudence the New Cool?" *The Huffington Post*, June 5, 2009, http://www.huffingtonpost.com /lisa-earle-mcleod/teen-trends-is-fiscal-pru_b_196735.html.

16. Henry David Thoreau, https://www.walden.org/Library/Quotations /Simplicity.

17. Margot Starbuck, "Stockpiling Treasures in My Junk Closet," *Christianity Today*, November 2014, http://www.christianitytoday .com/women/2014/november/stockpiling-treasures-in-my-junk -closet.html?paging=off.

18. John Ortberg, *When the Game Is Over, It All Goes Back in the Box* (Grand Rapids, Michigan; Zondervan, 2007), 14.

19. Richard I. Kirkland Jr., "Should You Leave It All to the Children?" *Fortune*, September 29, 1986, http://archive.fortune.com/magazines /fortune/fortune_archive/1986/09/29/68098/index.htm.

20. "The Use of Money," II, 6, 7.

21. Ibid., I, 8.

22. Stephen R. Covey, *The 7 Habits of Highly Effective People: Powerful Lessons in Personal Change* (New York: Simon & Schuster, 1989, 2004), Part Two, Habit 2, https://www.stephencovey .com/7habits/7habits-habit2.php.

Chapter 4: Give All You Can

1. Tennessee Williams, *Cat on a Hot Tin Roof* (Sewanee, Tennessee: The University of the South, 1954, 1955, 1982, 1983, 2004), Act Two, 88.

2. Ibid., 91.

3. John Wesley, "The Danger of Riches," Sermon 87, II, 10, http://www .umcmission.org/Find-Resources/John-Wesley-Sermons/Sermon -87-The-Danger-of-Riches#sthash.FuSKKWTQ.dpuf.

4. "The Use of Money," III, 1.

5. David Gibson, "Rendering unto God," *Faith & Leadership*, March 3, 2009, http://www.faithandleadership.com/features/articles/rendering- unto-god.

6. William Sloane Coffin, The *Collected Sermons of William Sloane Coffin: The Riverside Years, Vol. 1* (Louisville: John Knox Press, 2008), 125.

7. Collection on Selina Hastings, Countess of Huntingdon, Southern Methodist University, Texas Archival Resources Online, http://www.lib.utexas.edu/taro/smu/00222/smu-00222.html.

8. Paul Collier, "'A Path Appears,' by Nicholas Kristof and Sheryl WuDunn," Sunday Book Review, *The New York Times*, October 16, 2014, http://www.nytimes.com/2014/10/19/books/review/a-path-appears-by-nicholas-kristof-and-sheryl-wudunn.html?_r=0.

9. Charles Dickens, *A Christmas Carol: A Ghost Story of Christmas* (London: Bradbury and Evans, 1858), Stave V, "The End of It."

10. "The Use of Money," III, 3.

11. James A. Harnish, *A Disciple's Heart: Growing in Love and Grace* (Nashville: Abingdon, 2015).

12. "The Use of Money," Intro, 2.

13. *The Collected Sermons of William Sloane Coffin*, Vol. 2, 72.

14. Ibid., 73.

15. Ibid., 74.

16. C. S. Lewis, *Mere Christianity* (San Francisco: HarperSanFrancisco, 2009), 135.